ANNIE'S ROMANTIC LIVING
Christmas™

Product Development Director
Andy Ashley

Publishing Services Manager
Ange Van Arman

Product Development Manager
Marilyn Shelton

Product Development Staff
**Mickie Akins, Darla Hassell, Sandra Miller Maxfield,
Alice Mitchell, Elizabeth Ann White**

Editor
Nancy Harris

Assistant Editors
Donna Jones, Michelle Hudson

Book Design
Diane Simpson

Graphic Artist
Minette Smith

Production Artist
Debby Keel

Photography Supervisor
Scott Campbell

Photographers
Andy J. Burnfield, Tammy Payne

Photo Stylist
Martha Coquat

Photo Assistant
Salway Sabri

Production Assistant
Glenda Chamberlain

Copyright ® 2001 Annie's Attic.
All rights reserved. No part of this book may
be reproduced in any form or by any means
without the written permission of the product development
director, excepting brief quotations
in connection with reviews written specifically
for inclusion in magazines, newspapers
and other publications.

Library of Congress Cataloging-in-Publication Data
ISBN: 0-9655269-8-4
First Printing: 2001
Library of Congress Catalog Card Number: 00-133624
Published and Distributed by
Annie's Attic, Big Sandy, Texas 75755
AnniesAttic.com
Printed in the United States of America

Dear Fellow Crafters,

I have wonderful memories of the Christmas mornings of my childhood, but I find that I enjoy the holiday more with every passing year!

I'm not referring to the commercial season, or even the sights and sounds traditionally associated with the holiday. I am talking about the time of year when we can share with our loved ones the joy and affection that we feel for each of them.

The spirit of Christmas is truly the essence of giving, not only of fresh-baked goodies or beautifully wrapped packages, but especially in handmade gifts offered with love.

Open your heart this holiday season to those you love most, as well as to those less fortunate. When you do, it's guaranteed to make this Christmas the most satisfying one of your life!

Happy Holidays,

Annie

TABLE OF Contents

CHAPTER ONE
Tree Trims

Velvet Star Ornaments.............. 8
Beaded Christmas
   Decorations........................ 10
Snowman Light Covers 14
Copper Ornaments.................. 16
Gold Christmas Star................ 18
Victorian Christmas Tree Skirt
   and Kissing Ball Ornament.. 20
Painted Ornaments.................. 24
Floral Grape Ornaments.......... 30
Angel Tree Topper................... 32
Crystal Prisms........................ 34
Impressed Velvet Tree Skirt..... 36
Ribbon Rose Ornament 42

CHAPTER TWO
Entertaining Delights

Ornament Place Cards 46
Bow and Holly Mosaic Tray 48
Christmas Appetizers 50
Holly Tray and Chargers 50
Frozen Holiday Ice Bucket.......... 51
Christmas Card Tea Tray
   and Coaster 56
Christmas Dinner...................... 58
Wired Poinsettia Table Set.......... 59
Luminarias 64
Beaded Evening Bag 66
Five Golden Rings Table Wreath .. 68
Christmas Desserts 70
Old-World Finial Topiary
   and Candleholders 71
Peppermint Candy Boxes........... 80

CHAPTER THREE
Gifts Galore

Clay Bible Cover	84
Gift Tubes and Jewelry	86
Cookie Food Gifts	88
Christmas Greeting Cards	90
Old-World Santa Pin	95
Braided Necklaces	96
Bottle Gift Bags	98
Towel Rose Gift Box	102
Victorian Christmas Basket	104
Santa's Magic Key	107
Holiday Bird Feeder and Birdhouse	108
Sweet Indulgence	110
Christmas Potpourri Pillow	114
Candles	116

CHAPTER FOUR
Holiday Home

Embossed Felt Mantle Scarf	120
Victorian Christmas Boxes	122
Glass Ornament Wreath	124
Santa Claus	126
Christmas Floral Trio Set	130
Holiday Borders	134
Victorian Stocking	136
Kissing Ball	140
Christmas Books	142
Wooden Cross	144
Gold Nativity Set	146
Christmas Doormat	148
Poinsettia Glass Clings	150
Victorian Christmas Wall Hanging	152
Poinsettia Flower Box	154
Christmas Tassels	158

CHAPTER ONE
Tree Trims

From the dazzling trims to the graceful elegance of angels, you'll discover a treasure of creative Yuletide adornments for the evergreen, as well as the home.

Velvet Star Ornaments

Designed by Brenda Spitzer

Materials for Set of Three:
- 48"-wide "Fidelio" Velvet by J.B. Martin ($\frac{1}{6}$ yd. of each color):
  - $\frac{1}{6}$ yd. of Brandy #5762
  - $\frac{1}{6}$ yd. of Smokestone #4679
  - $\frac{1}{6}$ yd. of Dark Olive #5592
- 3 star-shaped 5"-diameter paper maché ornaments
- White Washout Marking Pencil #680 by Wrights®
- Pkg. of 3 mm iridescent seed beads
- 18" piece of thin gold cord
- Terry cloth bath towel and hand towel
- Sewing needle and matching threads
- Aluminum foil
- Distilled water
- Spray bottle
- Steam iron
- Scissors
- Fabri-Tac™ by Beacon™ or fabric glue

Instructions

1: For each star, lay the fabric wrong side up on a flat work surface, place two of the paper maché ornaments at one short end of the fabric; using the white marking pencil, draw an outline around each ornament $\frac{1}{4}$" larger on all edges than the ornaments; cut out. Repeat with each remaining piece of fabric.

2: From each piece of velvet fabric, cut a strip 1" wide x 17" long.

3: Fold the bath towel in half and place it on a hard work surface for ironing. Fill the iron with distilled water and heat on medium setting. Place **one star** of each color fabric and the three long strips of fabric right side up on the towel; lightly spray each of the fabric pieces with water.

4: Crumple up several sheets of the aluminum foil, smooth them out just a bit, then cover each of the fabric pieces with the foil.

5: To impress the foil texture into the fabric, moisten the hand towel with water and wring out well; place the hand towel over the foil and fabric layers. Using the iron, apply heavy pressure and press one area for 20 seconds; lift the iron, press down on a new area for 20 seconds. Continue this process until all of the fabric pieces have been pressed. Remove the hand towel and the foil. If more impression and texture is desired, replace the foil, cover with the moistened hand towel and repeat the pressing process for an additional 15 seconds on each area. When desired texture has been achieved, remove the foil and hand towel and allow fabric pieces to dry.

6: With the sewing needle and matching thread, sew 50 to 60 seed beads randomly across the right side of each impressed star, leaving $\frac{1}{2}$" around the edges uncovered.

7. With the scissors, make a $\frac{1}{4}$" cut at each inside corner on each of the six fabric stars.

8: To **cover the back** of each ornament, lay an unimpressed fabric star wrong side up on the work surface and center one of the paper maché ornaments over each fabric star. Run a thin bead of glue around the exposed edges of the fabric star; fold the exposed edges of the fabric up to cover the side of the ornament and press in place; let dry.

9: In the same manner, **cover the front** of the ornaments using the matching-color impressed fabric star; let dry.

10: For the **ornament hangers**, cut the gold cord into three pieces each 6" long. Fold one piece of gold cord in half and glue the ends of the cord to one side of a point on one star. Repeat for each ornament.

11: Lay the long fabric strips out on the work surface with the wrong sides up. Fold the long sides on each fabric strip $\frac{1}{4}$" to wrong side and glue in place. Fold over one short side of each fabric strip $\frac{1}{4}$" and glue in place.

12: To **cover the sides** of each ornament, using the matching color fabric strip, glue the folded short end of the strip to the side of the ornament covering the hanger ends; gluing as you go, continue to wrap the fabric strip around the ornament sides to the first point. Allowing $\frac{1}{4}$" for the hem, cut the fabric strip to fit; fold the last end of the fabric strip under $\frac{1}{4}$" and glue in place. Let dry.

❊ Tips for Decorating Your Tree

First, whether you are using a natural or artificial tree, reshape the tree. Think of how a tree grows, with each frond leaning towards the sun, and work from bottom to top and back to front, giving each branch a lift up and out.

Next, add lights—the more the merrier! For light coverage, use 150 lights per foot of tree, for moderate coverage, 200 lights per foot and for an all-out glow, 250 lights per foot of tree. The new "light webs" are easiest to use, or weave strings of lights from trunk to tip and back again. Or string lights like garlands, horizontally or vertically, for a different effect.

Finally, add decorations and garlands. Start with bows, ribbons and larger ornaments, and fill in with smaller ornaments and silk flowers.

Beaded Christmas Decorations

Designed by Marilyn Shelton

Beaded Garland

Finished Size:
Each scallop is 9" across at the top.

Materials for One Scallop (see Note below):
- Silver Washed #127 Beads by The Beadery®:
    - 26 Silver 4 mm Round #702
    - 18 Silver 5 mm Round #703
    - 30 Silver 6 mm Round #705
    - 6 Silver 8 mm Round #715
    - 8 Silver 10 mm Round #716
    - 6 Silver 12 mm Round #717
    - 6 Silver 14 mm Round #718
    - 3 Silver 18 mm Round #721
    - 6 Silver 6 x 9 mm Oat #1124
    - 6 Silver 6 x 19 mm Spaghetti #770
    - 2 Silver 9 x 10 mm Barrel #1112
- Spool of 24-gauge Silver Wire #2490-218 by The Beadery®
- Bead Design Board #469-11 by Mangelsen's
- Bead sorting tray or small bowls
- Jewelry Designer™ Tools Kit #1893-09 by Darice®

Note: Additional materials will be needed for each Scallop desired.

Instructions

1: Pour the beads into separate sections of the sorting tray or small bowls. On the bead board, arrange the beads in order according to Scallop Pattern illustration.
2: For the **beginning section** of beads, string on one barrel bead; to **secure** the end of the wire, with the jewelry pliers, wrap the end around the bead and up through the hole two times, leaving a 4" end. String on ten 4 mm beads and one 10 mm bead *(see End Beads illustration)*.

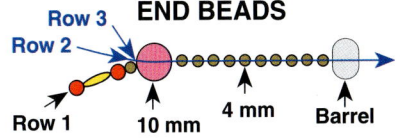

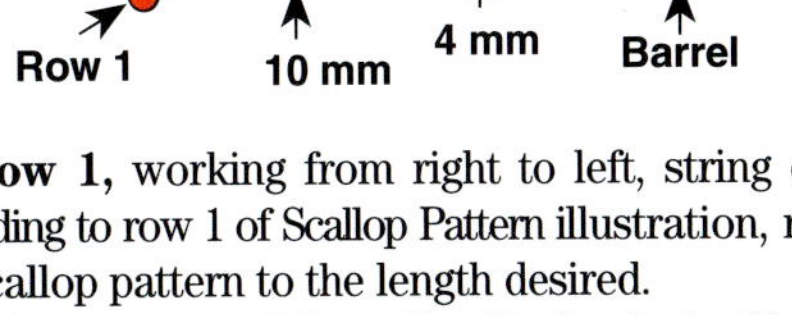

END BEADS

3: For **row 1**, working from right to left, string on beads according to row 1 of Scallop Pattern illustration, repeating the scallop pattern to the length desired.
4: When the first row of the garland is the desired length, for the **finishing section** of beads, string on ten 4 mm beads

Continued on page 12

Beaded Christmas Decorations

Continued from page 11

and one barrel bead. In the same manner as step 2, **secure** the end of the wire by wrapping it around and through the 10 mm bead two times. Leaving a 4" end, cut off any excess wire with the wire cutters.

5: For **row 2**, with a separate length of wire, string one end of the wire through the first 10 mm bead on row 1, through the next ten 4 mm beads and through the barrel bead *(see blue line in End Beads illustration)*. Secure the wire as before, leaving a 4" end.

6: Working from right to left with the other end of the wire, string the beads according to the Scallop Pattern for row 2, threading the wire through each corresponding 10 mm dividing bead at the end of each scallop on row 1.

7: At the end of the last scallop on row 2, thread the end of the wire through the last ten 4 mm beads, through the barrel bead and **secure** as before.

8: Following the Scallop Pattern, work row 3 in the same manner as row 2.

9: With the pliers, twist the 4" wire ends together as one on each end of the garland, fold the wire in half, forming a hanging loop at the fold *(see Hanging Loop illustration)*, twist the end of the wire around the base of the hanging loop several times to secure.

HANGING LOOP

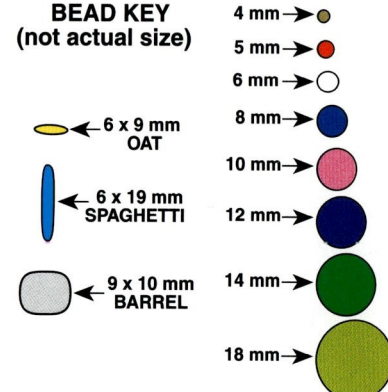

Beaded Snowflakes

Finished Sizes:
Sizes range from 5¾" to 7".

Materials for Three:
- Silver Washed #127 Beads by The Beadery®:
  - 12 Silver 4 mm Round #702
  - 12 Silver 5 mm Round #703
  - 24 Silver 6 mm Round #705
  - 6 Silver 8 mm Round #715
  - 12 Silver 10 mm Round #716
  - 12 Silver 12 mm Round #717
  - 6 Silver 14 mm Round #718
  - 2 Silver 13 mm Round Cabochons #X663
  - 4 Silver 11 mm Round Cabochons #X662
  - 12 Silver 6 x 9 mm Oat #1124
  - 30 Silver 8 x 9 mm Mushroom #936
  - 6 Silver 8 x 12 mm Oval #993
  - 6 Silver 10 x 18 mm Oval #995
  - 30 Silver 6 mm Rondelle #740
  - 6 Silver 6 x 19 mm Spaghetti #770
- Bead Design Board #469-11 by Mangelsen's *(optional)*
- 24-gauge Silver Wire #2490-218 by The Beadery®
- Jewelry Designer™ Tools Kit #1893-09 by Darice®
- Crafty® Magic Melt® Oval Magic Pro Glue Gun by Adhesive Technologies, Inc.
- Crafty® Magic Melt® Jewelry Glue by Adhesive Technologies, Inc.

Basic Instructions

1: For each Snowflake, cut three pieces of wire each 12" long.

2: Lay a cabochon on the work surface with the flat side up. Place a drop of glue in the center of the cabochon and lay three wires across the center *(see red lines on the Wire Placement illustration)*. Place a drop of glue on top of the wires where they cross and place a matching cabochon, flat side down, on top of the wires; let glue dry.

3: Following the diagram for each Snowflake, arrange the beads on the bead board; string the beads onto each wire as indicated. After the last bead has been added to each wire, with the pliers, bend the end of the wire around the last bead and back up through the hole of the last bead to secure the end. Trim any excess wire.

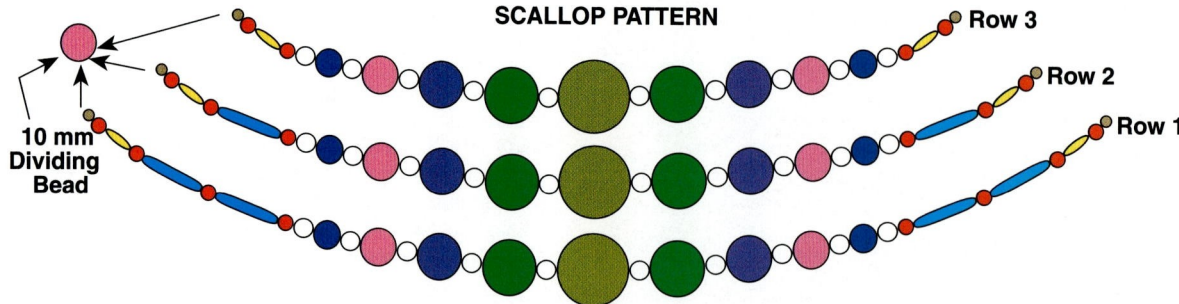

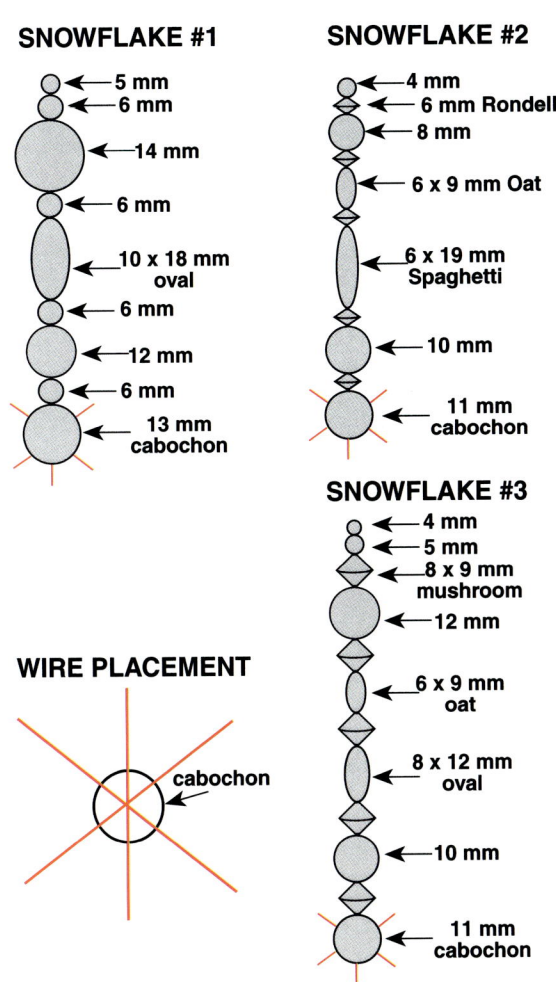

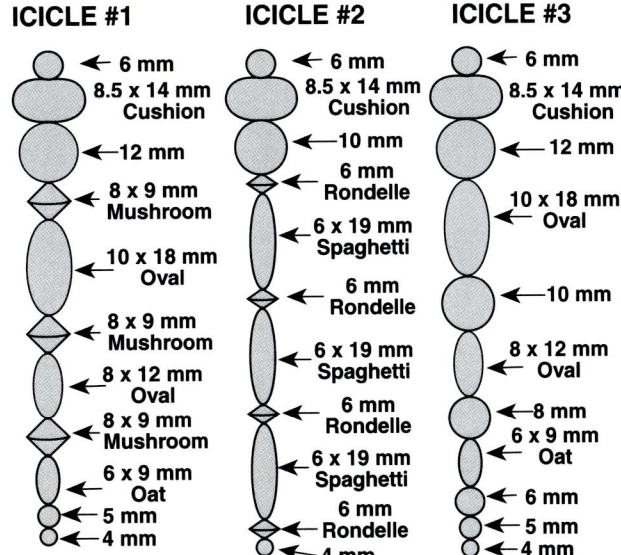

Beaded Icicles

Finished Sizes:
Sizes range from 3½" to 4".

Materials for Three:
❑ Silver Washed #127 Beads by The Beadery®:
   3 Silver 4 mm Round #702
   2 Silver 5 mm Round #703
   4 Silver 6 mm Round #705
   Silver 8 mm Round #715
   Silver 10 mm Round #716
   Silver 12 mm Round #717
   Silver 14 mm Round #718
   2 Silver 6 x 9 mm Oat #1124
   3 Silver 8 x 9 mm Mushroom #936
   Silver 8 x 12 mm Oval #993
   Silver 10 x 18 mm Oval #995
   40 Silver 6 mm Rondelle #740
   3 Silver 6 x 19 mm Spaghetti #770
❑ 24-gauge Silver Wire #2490-218 by The Beadery®
❑ Jewelry Designer™ Tools Kit #1893-09 by Darice®

Instructions
1: For each Icicle, cut a 12" piece of wire. For the **hanging loop,** loosely fold the piece of wire in half; about ¼" from the fold, twist the wire together to form a loop *(see Twisted Hanging Loop illustration)*.
2: Holding the two wires together as one, string the beads onto both wires according to each individual Icicle diagram. After the last bead has been added to each Icicle, bend the end of one wire around the last bead and back up through the hole to secure the end. Trim any excess wire.

Beaded Tassels

Finished Sizes:
Sizes range from 3½" to 4".

Materials for Three:
❑ Silver Washed #127 Beads by The Beadery®:
   16 Silver 4 mm Round #702
   32 Silver 5 mm Round #703
   112 Silver 6 mm Round #705
   3 Silver 10 mm Round #716
   24 Silver 6 x 19 mm Spaghetti #770
   72 Silver 6 x 9 mm Oat #1124
   3 Silver 8.5 x 14 mm Cushion #1115
❑ 24-gauge Silver Wire #2490-218 by The Beadery®
❑ Jewelry Designer™ Tools Kit #1893-09 by Darice®

Instructions
1: For each Tassel, cut four pieces of wire each 12" long. For the **hanging loop,** holding all four pieces of wire together as one, loosely fold the wire in half; about ¼" from the fold, twist the wire together to form a loop *(see Twisted Hanging Loop illustration)*.
2: For the **top of each Tassel,** holding all eight wires together as one, thread on a 10 mm round bead and one cushion bead.
3: With the hanging loop held at the bottom, spread the eight wires apart slightly. Working with just one wire at a time, string the Tassel beads *(gray beads in Tassel diagrams)* onto each wire according to the appropriate diagram. After the last bead has been added to each wire, bend the end of the wire around the last bead and back up through the hole to secure the end. Trim any excess wire. ❈

Continued on page 31

Snowman Light Covers

Designed by Dorris Sorensen

Finished Sizes:
Each Light Cover is 2¼" x 2½".

Materials:
- Air-Dry PermEnamel™ Liquid Lead™ #457900201 by Delta Technical Coatings, Inc.
- Air-Dry PermEnamel™ Transparent Glass Paint™ by Delta Technical Coatings, Inc.:
  - White #457100202
  - Kelly Green #457040202
  - Yellow #457060202
  - Red #457030202
- String of clear miniature lights
- Toothpick
- Tracing paper
- Transparent tape
- Pencil
- Several spring-type clothes pins
- Large piece of heavy cardboard
- Plastic wrap
- Iron and pressing cloth
- Large book to press Light Covers *(phone book, dictionary)*

Instructions

1: Trace enough Light Cover Patterns onto tracing paper to cover each light on your light string. Lay the traced patterns on the piece of cardboard and tape in it place. Cover the entire surface of the cardboard with plastic wrap, pulling the plastic wrap tight and smoothing all wrinkles; tape in place.

Note: Before using the liquid lead and glass paints, turn the bottle upside down and gently tap the bottle four or five times on a hard surface. This will send the air bubbles to the top and will allow the paint and liquid lead to flow smoothly.

2: With the liquid lead, fill in the snowman's eyes and trace over all of the pattern lines (including the mouth) of both the front and back of the snowman head, joining them in the center with the light ring *(make sure the center of the light ring is left open)*. Let dry completely.

3: With the red and green glass paints, fill in the leaded areas of the hat and hatband. With the white paint, fill in the face and back of the head, working around the eyes, nose and mouth. Mix a drop of red and a drop of yellow in the leaded nose area and blend together with a toothpick to get orange. Let dry overnight.

4: Gently peel each Light Cover off of the plastic-covered cardboard and place between the pages of a large book to press flat. Leave the Light Covers in the book for seven to ten days to allow the paint to cure.

5: Remove the Light Covers from the book. With the iron on medium heat, place a press cloth over one Light Cover at a time and gently iron it until it is soft and pliable.

6: While the Light Cover is still warm, fold it in half, matching the edges of the head and hat. To bond the two sides of the Light Cover together, run a bead of liquid lead around the edges of the entire head and hat; clip each side with a clothespin until dry.

7: Remove the clothespins and insert the miniature lightbulb through the center of the light ring.

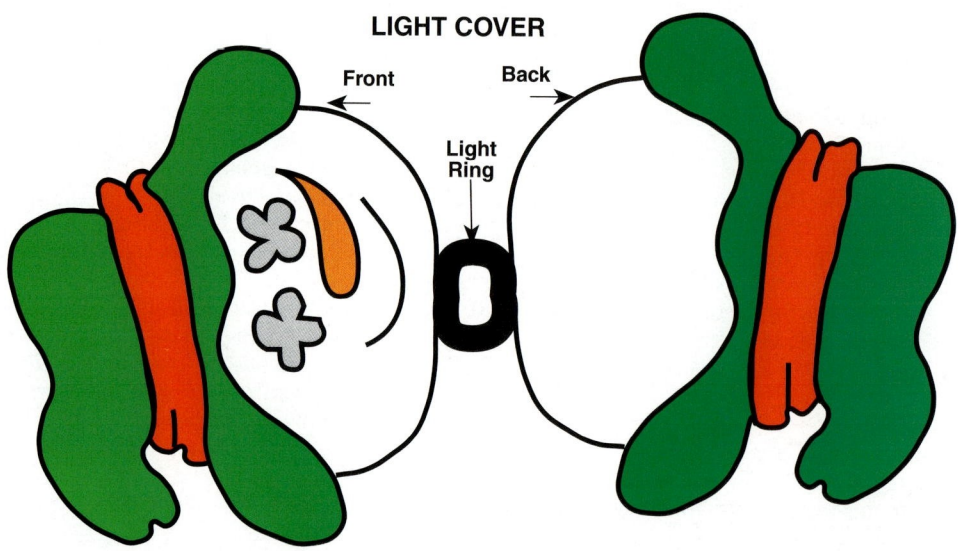

LIGHT COVER

Copper Ornaments

Designed by Delores F. Ruzicka

Finished Sizes:
Ornaments sizes range from 4" to 5½" long.

Materials for Set of Six:
- 8½" x 12" piece of medium-weight Copper Tooling Foil by Amaco®
- Liver of sulphur *(antiquing agent found in craft stores)*
- 4" x 6" piece of desired color cardstock for each ornament
- 48" gold cord
- ½"-wide gold foil star
- Steel wool
- Tracing paper
- Pencil
- Transparent tape
- Scissors or small tin shears
- Decorative-edged scissors
- Stylus or non-working ball-point pen
- Pad of old newspapers *(about 1"-thick)*
- 1/16" Hole Punch #532 by McGill®
- Crafter's Pick™ Ultimate Tacky Glue by The Adhesive Products, Inc.

Instructions

1: Trace each of the patterns onto tracing paper *(see page 29 for other patterns)*, including all of the detailing on the patterns.
2: Place the patterns on the foil and tape it in place; lay the sheet of foil on top of the thick pad of newspaper to cushion the foil.
3: To **tool the front** of the ornaments, use the stylus or non-working pen to firmly trace over the pattern lines and make an impression in the foil, transferring the pattern. **Do not trace** over the criss-cross lines of the Angel's wings and the Candy Cane, the snowflakes on the Christmas Tree or the wavy lines around the Gingerbread Boy and the Gingerbread Girl. Remove the paper pattern and trace over the lines on the foil again if desired for more definition.
4: With the decorative scissors, cut out the Partridge ornament. Cut out all other ornaments with regular scissors.
5: To **tool the back** of the ornaments, tape the Angel, the Candy Cane, the Christmas Tree and the Gingerbread Boy and Girl patterns to the back side of the appropriate foil cutouts. In the same manner as before, tool the criss-cross lines on the Angel's wings and the Candy Cane, tool the wavy lines around the Gingerbread Boy and Girl and tool the snowflakes on the Tree.
6: If desired, the year can be added to each ornament by tooling the numbers directly onto the front of the ornament.
7: To **antique the ornaments,** following the manufacturer's instructions, apply the liver of sulphur to each ornament. Using the steel wool, remove as much or as little of the liver of sulphur from the ornaments as needed to achieve the desired look.
8: To **mount the ornaments** on the cardstock, apply an even layer of glue to the back of each ornament; center the ornament on the cardstock and press in place. Let dry.
9: With the decorative scissors, trim the cardstock around the Partridge, leaving a 1/16" border all around. In the same manner, using regular scissors, trim around the remaining ornaments.
10: Glue the gold foil star to the front of the Angel *(see photo)*.
11: With the hole punch, punch a hole in the top of each ornament for hanging.
12: For each **hanger** *(make 6),* cut an 8"-long piece of gold cord. Insert one end of the cord through the hole in the top of one ornament; matching the ends of the cord, tie a knot about 1" from the end.

GINGERBREAD BOY

Continued on page 29

Gold Christmas Star

Designed by Phyllis Dobbs

Finished Size:
7" across.

Materials:
- ⅓ yd. of solid gold fabric
- 6" x 12" piece of coordinating gold print fabric
- 5 yds. of Aztec Gold #202HL size 32 Heavy Braid by Kreinik Mfg. Co.
- Pkg. of Ice #02010 Mill Hill Seed Beads by Gay Bowles Sales
- 10" of ⅛" Gold Braid by Wrights® *(gold cord)*
- Soft Stuff Fiberfill by The Warm™ Company
- 62 silver-lined size E rocaille beads
- ½" white moon button
- Sewing needle
- Beading needle
- Embroidery needle
- White beading thread
- Air soluble disappearing ink pen
- Scissors
- Straight pins
- Ruler
- Tracing paper
- Pencil
- Sewing machine *(optional)*

Instructions *(See page 23 for all patterns, diagrams and illustrations)*

1: Trace the Star Points pattern onto tracing paper and cut out. Cut three Star Points from the solid fabric and three from the print fabric.
2: For the **front of the Star,** allowing ¼" seam allowance and alternating fabrics, sew three Points together to form the top half of the Star; sew three points together to form the bottom half of the Star; sew the two halves together.

Note: The embroidery stitches on the Star points can be worked freehand or, if desired, use the disappearing ink pen to mark the placement of the stitches and beads using the Embroidery Diagram as a guide.

3: For **stitching the solid gold points** of the Star *(green lines on Embroidery Diagram),* thread the embroidery needle with heavy gold braid and sew long straight stitches to outline the piece leaving a ¼" border all around. For the grid pattern inside the outline, evenly space four long straight stitches on the diagonal.
4: With the embroidery needle and heavy gold braid, stitch cross-stitches over each intersection to secure the straight stitches *(see red X's on Embroidery Diagram).*
5: With the sewing needle and a double strand of beading thread, sew one E bead at the center of each space on the grid.
6: For **stitching the gold print points** of the Star *(see green lines on Embroidery Diagram),* work step 1 of the Lazy Daisy stitch, thread on one E bead and complete step 2 of the stitch.
7: With the sewing needle and a double strand of beading thread, sew the moon button to the center of all the Star points.
8: For the **back of the Star,** with right sides together, pin the front of the Star to the remaining piece of the solid gold fabric. Cut out around the Star front.
9: For the **hanger,** fold the 10" piece of gold cord in half, place the folded cord between the two layers of the Star with the ends of the cord at the tip of one point and the loop of the cord in the center of the Star, pin in place.
10: Allowing ¼" for seams all around, sew the front and back together, leaving 1½" open along the side of one point for stuffing. Clip the inside corners up to the seam line, trim the seam allowance above each point and turn the Star right side out. Firmly stuff the Star with fiberfill and sew the opening closed.
11: For the **seed bead fringe** at the top of the Star, thread the beading needle with one 36" strand of thread, tie a knot at one end of the thread and secure it to the Star just below the hanger. Thread on enough seed beads to form a 2" strand, thread on one E bead, push the beads up to the fabric; skipping over the E bead, insert the needle back through all of the seed beads, out the top of the first seed bead and through the fabric to secure. Repeat this process to create seven more strands of fringe in varying lengths between 1" and 2" long.
12: With the embroidery needle and a double strand of beading thread, sew one E bead to the end of each Star point *(see photo).*

Continued on page 23

❋ The Greatest Gift is You

Give an object of yours that someone has admired and attach a card with its history.

Present a gift certificate for a gift of your time: to run an errand or perform a task.

One thoughtful host gift-wrapped empty boxes, made a small slit in the top and labeled one for each guest. She supplied the guest with small slips of paper on which to write positive comments for every guest. As the boxes were passed from guest to guest, the messages were inserted in the appropriate boxes. The delighted guests would enjoy these boxes and the meaningful messages for years to come!

Victorian Christmas Tree Skirt and Kissing Ball Ornament

Designed by Beth Wheeler

Victorian Christmas Tree Skirt

Finished Size:
36" in diameter.

Materials:
- ❏ 1¼ yds. 45"-wide ecru cotton fabric
- ❏ 1¼ yds. 45"-wide white muslin
- ❏ 5 yds. gold ½"-wide shirred piping
- ❏ Assorted off-white and ecru crochet and Battenburg doilies in various sizes to cover top of Tree Skirt
- ❏ Assorted 1"-wide and 2"-wide sheer ribbons in coordinating colors
- ❏ 60 to 70 assorted buttons in matching colors
- ❏ Sewing needle
- ❏ Assorted threads to match fabric and ribbons
- ❏ Monofilament sewing thread
- ❏ Quilt basting spray adhesive
- ❏ Straight pins
- ❏ Scissors
- ❏ Ruler or yardstick
- ❏ Sewing machine

Instructions *(See page 22 for diagrams and illustrations)*

1: Fold the printed fabric as shown in the Folding diagram.

2: Cut the scalloped bottom edges of the printed fabric *(see dotted lines on Cutting illustrations)*, cut out the center circle and cut the side opening.

3: Using the printed fabric as a pattern, cut one from the muslin.

4: Starting in the center of one side opening, with the rolled edge of the piping toward the center of the printed fabric, matching edges, pin the piping to the right side of the fabric around the entire raw edge. Removing pins as you go, sew in place.

5: Matching edges, pin the printed fabric and muslin right sides together with piping between. Removing pins as you go and with stitches placed at the edge of the rolled piping, sew together leaving 10" open along one side opening for turning.

6: Clip all curves and corners as needed for Skirt to lay flat. Turn right side out.

7: With sewing needle and matching thread, sew the opening closed.

8: Lay the Tree Skirt out flat on the work surface with print side up. Experiment with the arrangement of the doilies on the Skirt, placing the largest ones first and working up to the smaller doilies.

9: When you are pleased with the arrangement, spray the backs of the doilies with the adhesive spray and adhere them in place on the Skirt.

10: Using the sewing machine set on a narrow zig-zag stitch and monofilament thread, sew the doilies in place.

11: For the large Ribbon Roses, cut a piece of the 2"-wide ribbon 3 yards long, fold the ribbon as shown in steps 1–5 of the Ribbon Roses illustration. Repeat steps 2–5 until all of the ribbon has been used and you have a compact packet of folded ribbon with two short tails.

12: Holding onto the tails, let go of the folded packet of ribbon and it will spring into a braided rope. Hold one tail securely and gently pull on the other tail to draw the ribbon up into a soft spiral. Do not pull the tail too far or the petals will be drawn into the center.

Continued on page 22

Tree Trims ~ page 21

Victorian Christmas Tree Skirt and Kissing Ball Ornament

Continued from page 21

13: With sewing needle and matching thread, sew the center of the ribbon rose to secure.

14: For the small ribbon roses, cut a piece of the 1"-wide ribbon 2 yards long. Fold and secure the same as for the large ribbon roses.

15: Sew roses in clusters at each scallop and one cluster at the center circle *(see photo)*.

16: For the **Leaves,** cut a 4"-long piece of 1"-wide ribbon, fold according to the Ribbon Leaves illustration. With needle and thread, run a gathering stitch across both tails, catching the straight edge of the ribbon behind as you go; pull thread to gather, secure. Sew around flower clusters as desired.

17: With needle and matching thread, sew buttons randomly around Tree Skirt and in the center of some roses *(see photo)*.

Kissing Ball Ornament

Finished Size:
4" in diameter excluding trims.

Materials:
- 4" diameter plastic Christmas ornament
- 12" round ecru crochet doily
- 10" piece of 1/8"-wide gold ribbon
- Assorted 1"-wide and 2"-wide sheer ribbons in coordinating colors *(for Ribbon Roses)*
- Assorted pearl shank buttons
- Gold spray paint
- Sewing needle and coordinating threads
- Ruler or yardstick
- Low temp glue gun and glue sticks *(optional)*

Instructions

1: Apply a light coat of gold spray paint to the plastic ornament; let dry. Apply additional coats as necessary for complete coverage.

2: With sewing needle and double strand of thread, run a gathering stitch around the outside edge of the doily; gently pull the thread to gather slightly. Place the plastic ornament inside the gathered doily with the hanging loop of

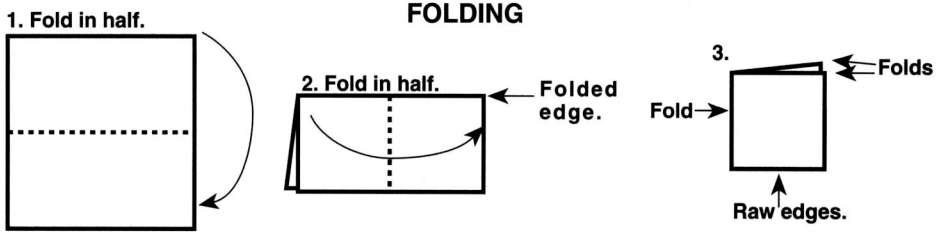

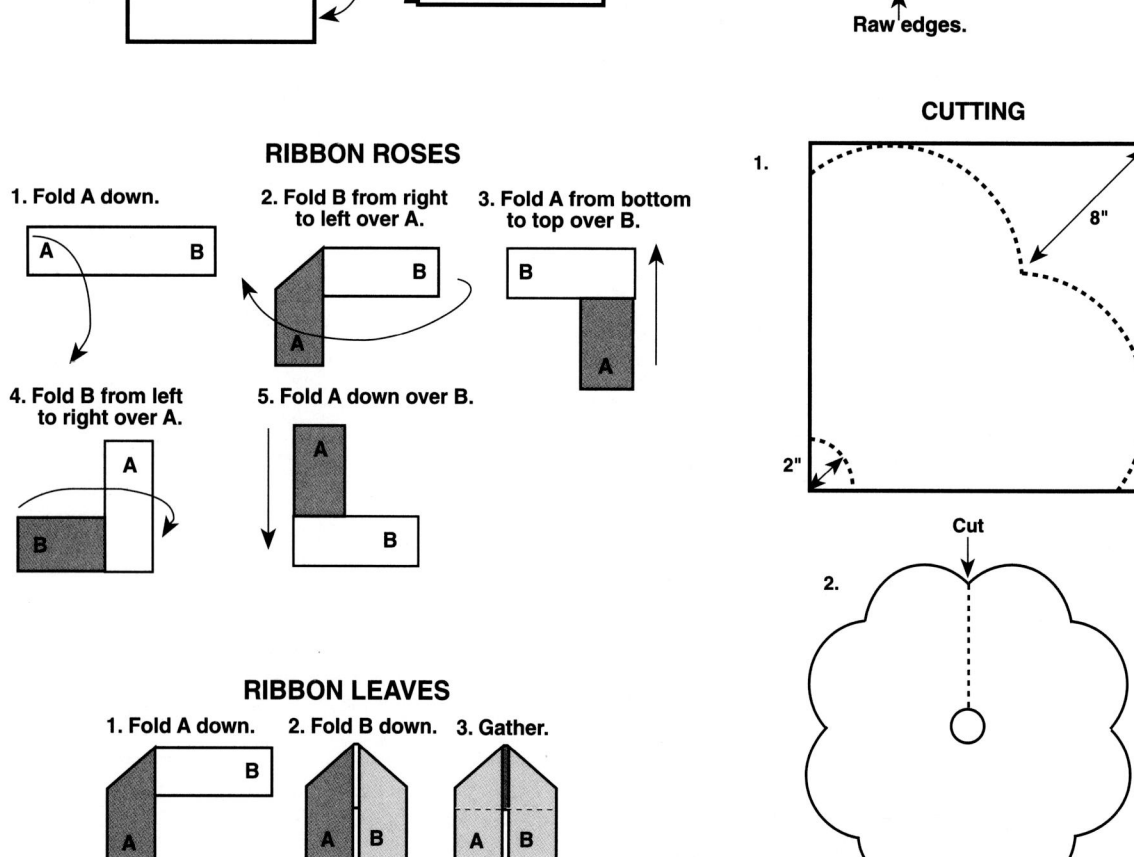

the ornament at the top; pull thread to gather and close the edges of the doily around the base of the hanging loop. Secure the thread around the hanging loop.

3: Make desired number of **Ribbon Roses** *(see Ribbon Roses illustrations)*; sew or glue roses in a cascade down one side of the ornament *(see photo)*.

4: Make the desired number of **Leaves** *(see Ribbon Leaves illustrations)*; cut a 4"-long piece of 1"-wide ribbon, fold according to the illustration. With needle and thread, run a gathering stitch across both tails, catching the straight edge of the ribbon behind as you go; pull thread to gather and secure. Sew around flower clusters as desired.

5: Thread one end of the ⅛"-wide gold ribbon through the hanging loop on the ornament; tie the ends of the ribbon together to form a loop.

Decoration Without Frustration

Nestle fresh fruit in with greenery; add candles for an easy, elegant arrangement.

Hang lovely holiday greeting cards to frame a doorway, mantle, stairway or pass-through.

Add festive bows to everything.

The glow of candles will tie your home decorating together when placed everywhere, even in the bathroom!

Gold Christmas Star
Continued from page 18

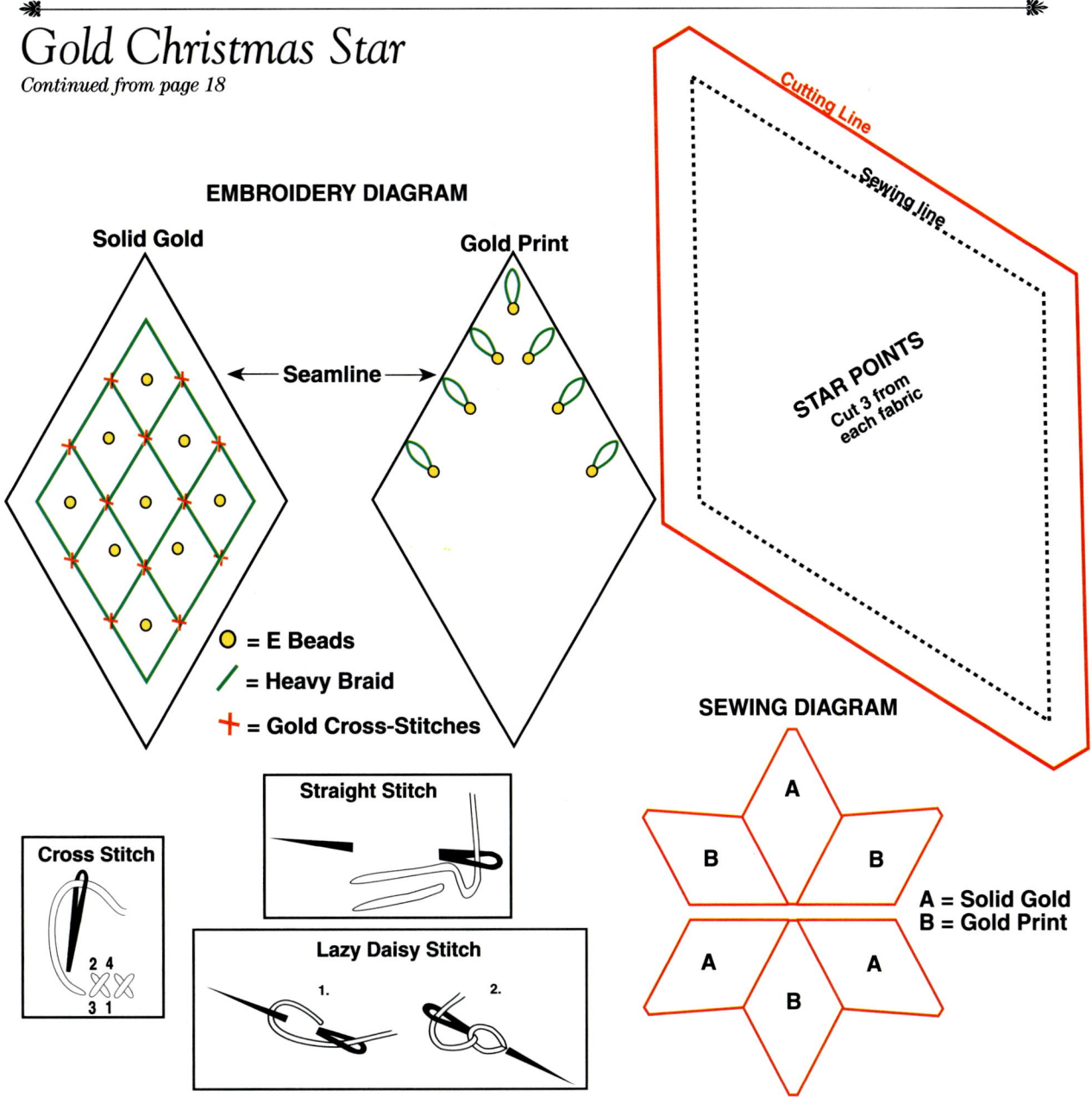

Tree Trims ~ page 23

Painted Ornaments

Designed by Kenna Prior

Finished Sizes:
Sizes range from 4¼" long to 5½" long.

Materials for All:
- Gallery Glass® products by Plaid®:
    - 2 pkgs. of Clear Styrene Blanks #16052
    - 2 pkgs. of Redi-Lead Strips #16089
    - Pkg. of Redi-Lead Circles #16090
    - 2 oz. bottle of Liquid Leading Grey #16078
- Gallery Glass® Window Color™ by Plaid®:
    - 4 oz. Gold Sparkle #16019
    - 4 oz. White Pearl #16021
    - 4 oz. Crystal Clear #16001
- 3½ yds. of gold cord *(for hangers)*
- Graphite Transfer Paper #1095 by Walnut Hollow
- Tracing paper
- Wooden toothpicks
- Wood Burning Tool with Stencil Tip #5580 by Walnut Hollow
- 24" square of scrap wood
- Pencil
- Scissors or craft knife
- Fabri-Tac™ by Beacon™ or craft glue

Instructions

1: Trace each of the patterns onto tracing paper *(see individual illustrations on pages 26, 27 and 28).* Place the graphite paper with the graphite side down on the scrap wood, lay one of the traced patterns on top of the graphite paper and retrace the **red** or **green** pattern lines to transfer the pattern to the wood. In the same manner, allowing about 1" all around each pattern, transfer the red lines of each pattern to the wood.

2: For each ornament, lay a styrene blank directly on the wood on top of one transferred pattern. With the wood burning tool and the stencil tip, following the manufacturer's instructions, trace around the transferred red pattern lines to cut out the ornament.

3: For the **hanger hole,** with the wood burning tool and the stencil tip, melt a small hole in the top of each ornament *(except the Harp and Letter).*

Note: When using the Redi-Lead to outline the different parts of each design, use the leading strips to outline the straight or slightly curved lines. For the circular or more sharply curved lines, choose one of the leading circles that closely matches the pattern line and trim the circle with scissors or a craft knife to fit that area.

4: To outline the pattern on the styrene cutouts, lay a paper pattern on the work surface and place the appropriate styrene cutout on top of the patterns. Following the manufacturer's instructions, apply the leading strips and lead circles to the styrene cutouts to outline the outer edges of the patterns first, then the inner lines. The center of a small leading circle is used for the Fish eye.

5: After all of the leading is completed, apply a drop of liquid lead at each joint where the leading meets, let dry.

6: Using the appropriate window colors *(see color keys and individual Patterns),* squeeze a generous amount of the window color into each section of the ornament, spreading the color with the tip of the bottle to fill in each section completely. If air bubbles form in the window color, use the tip of a toothpick to pop the bubbles and smooth out the color. If window color should get into the hanging hole, clean it out with a toothpick.

7: Curing time for the window color will vary depending on the weather and the amount of color used on each ornament. Allow the ornaments to dry and cure for at least two days or until they are no longer tacky feeling.

8: For the **Harp strings,** cut five pieces of gold cord each 6" long. Lay the cords across the Harp from top to bottom *(see gray dots on Harp Pattern)* and attach them to the Harp with a drop of glue on each grey dot; let dry. When the glue is completely dry, trim any excess cord close to the glue. Cover the end of each cord with a drop of liquid lead, let dry.

9: For each **hanger,** cut a piece of gold cord 9½" long. Fold the cord in half and tie the ends in a knot. Insert the fold through the hanger hole of each ornament *(except the Harp and Letter),* run the ends through the fold and pull to tighten. For the Harp and the Letter, insert the folded end of the cord through an opening at the top of the ornament, run the ends through the fold and pull to tighten.

Continued on page 26

❈ Symbols of Christmas – Yule Log

One of the most enduring traditions of Christmas in Europe is the lighting of the Yule Log. Family custom required the cutting of a large tree to find a log big enough to burn all through the twelve days of Christmas. The new log must be lit with a piece from the previous year's log and only by one with scrupulously clean hands (or the fire absolutely will not burn!). Ashes from the Yule Log were said to cure many diseases, and scrap pieces were kept for the next year's kindling, to ward off evil spirits.

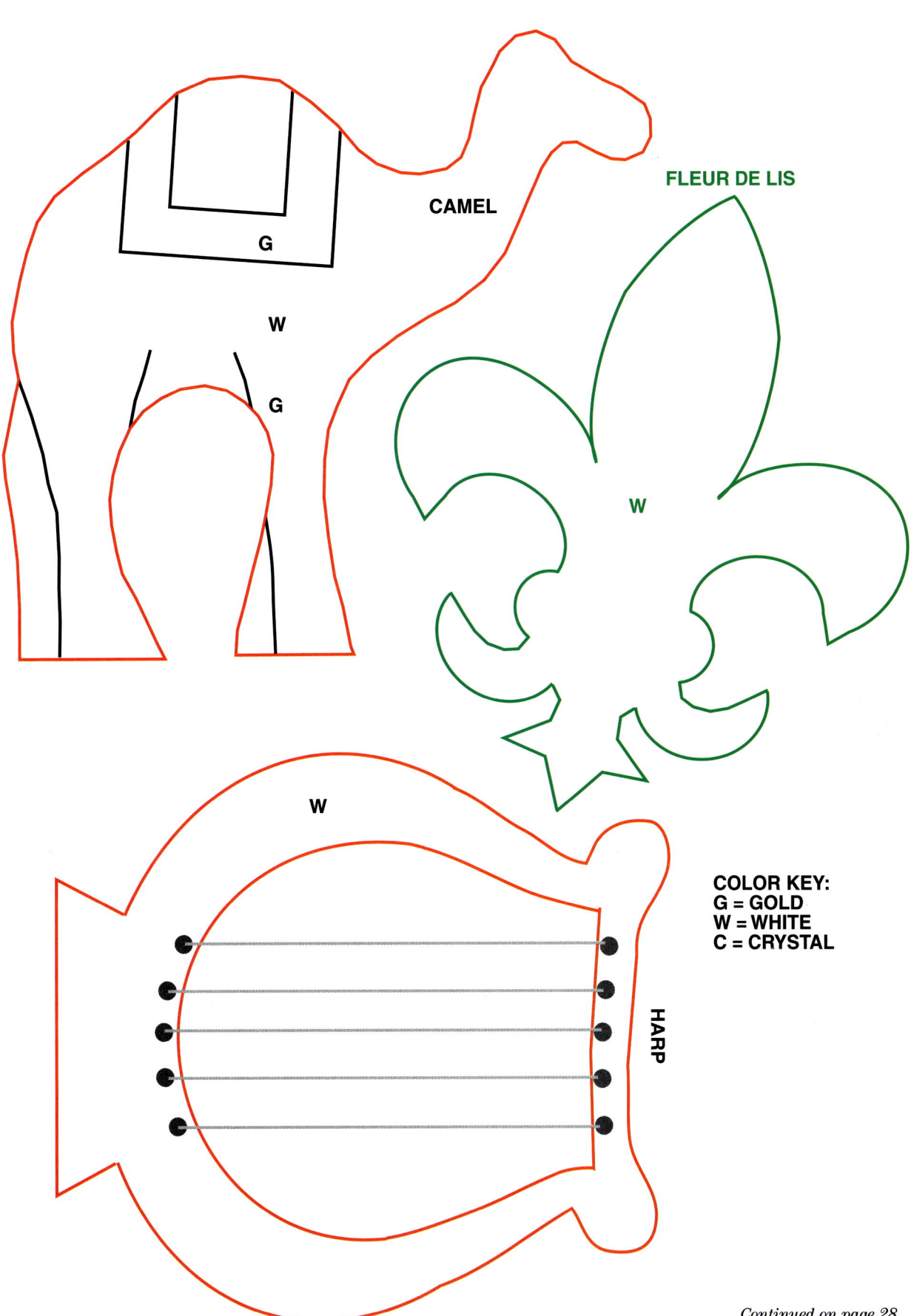

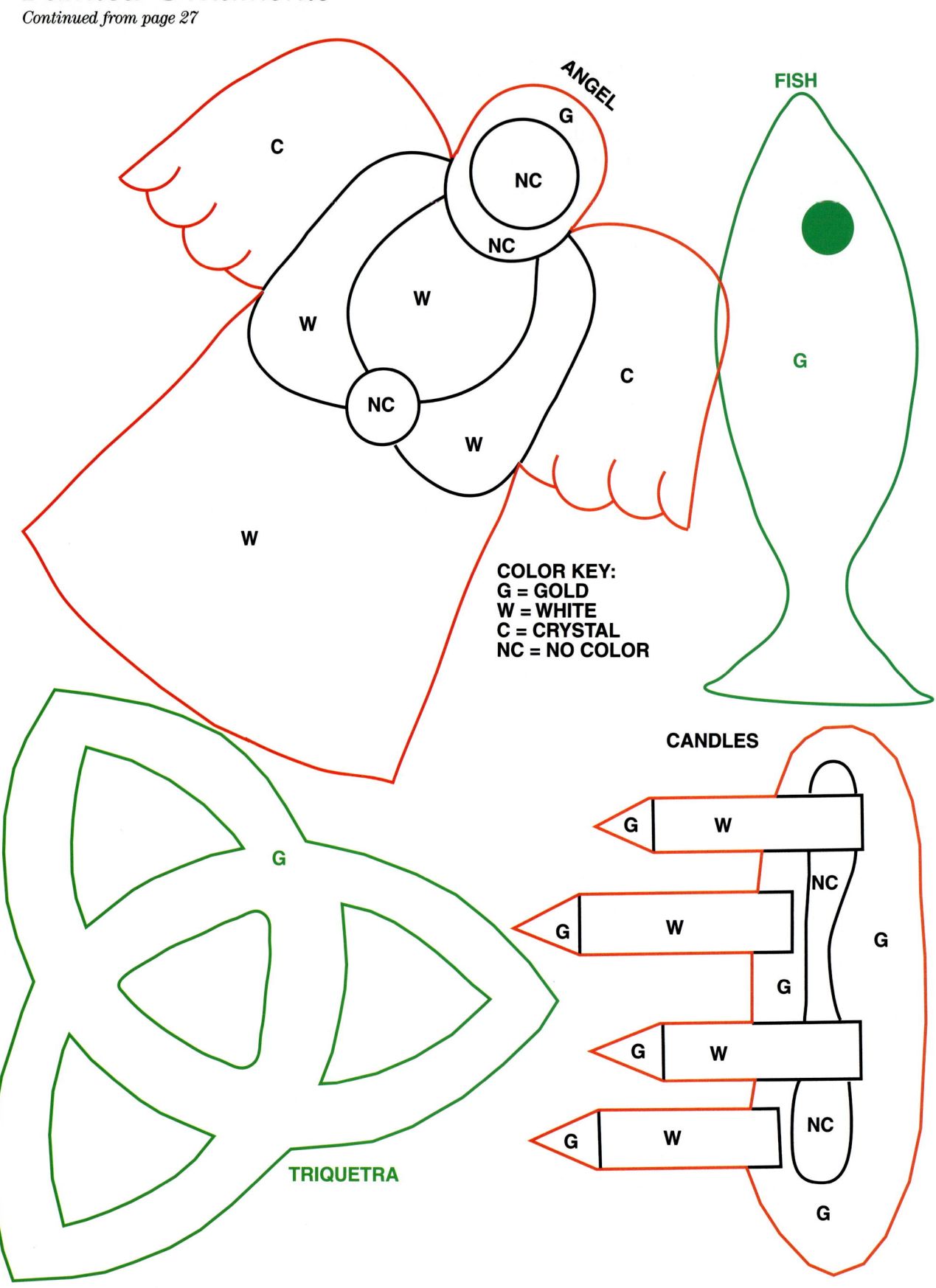

Copper Ornaments
Continued from page 17

GINGERBREAD GIRL

CHRISTMAS TREE

CANDY CANE

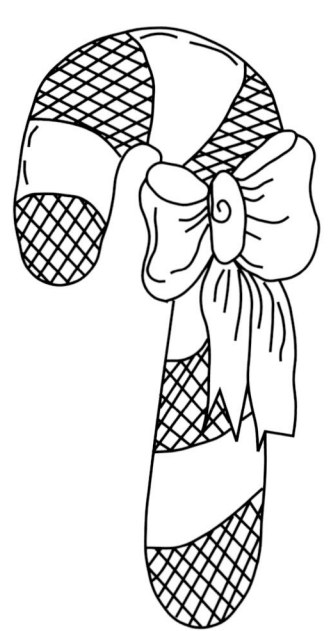

ANGEL

PARTRIDGE

Tree Trims ~ page 29

Floral Grape Ornaments

Designed by Kenna Prior

Finished Size:
About 6" long with florals.

Materials for Each:
- 3¼-diameter clear glass ornament
- Cluster of dark purple lilacs
- Cluster of small cream/rose flowers
- 2 stems of tiny white filler flowers
- Miniature grape cluster
- Dazzling Metallics™ Acrylic Paint by DecoArt™:
    Oyster Pearl #DA203
    Bronze #DA73
- Royal Metallics™ Brilliant Silver Textured Metallic Paint #DM04 by DecoArt™
- ½ yd. of purple/cream 1½"-wide wire edge ribbon
- 12" purple ¼"-wide satin ribbon
- 3" piece of fine-gauge wire
- Plastic or paper cup
- Wire cutters
- Crafty® Magic Melt® Oval Magic Pro Glue Gun by Adhesive Technologies, Inc.
- Crafty® Magic Melt® Glue Sticks by Adhesive Technologies, Inc.

Instructions

1: Carefully remove the metal cap and wire hanger from the ornament and set aside. Pour a quarter-sized puddle of each color paint into the opening of the ornament; slowly turn the ornament, swirling and mixing the paint colors until the inside of the ornament is completely covered. If necessary, add more paint and continue turning. Excess paint can be poured into another ball.

2: Place the ornament upside down in the top of a plastic or paper cup to drain excess paint and to dry completely. When dry, replace the metal cap and wire hanger in the top of the ornament.

3: Fold the 1½"-wide ribbon into a 5"-wide, single-loop bow and secure the center with the 3" piece of wire; trim wire ends. Cut the ends of the ribbon streamers in a "V" shape. Glue the bow to one side of the metal cap on the top of the ornament.

4: Thread one end of the ¼"-wide ribbon through the wire hanger and tie the ends in a knot to make a hanging loop.

5: Glue the stem of the grape cluster to the top of the ornament just behind the left loop of the bow with the grapes cascading down the side of the ornament *(see photo).*

6: With the wire cutters, separate all of the flowers and leaves into clusters of two or three each with stems about 1½" long. Glue the larger flowers around the top of the ornament, hiding the metal cap; use the smaller flowers and leaves to fill in any open areas.

Tree Alternatives

If there's no room for a large tree, or even a tree at all, consider hanging a well-constructed grouping of evergreen branches wired cleverly to a coathanger from a ceiling hook and decorate these as you would a tree.

Or if floor space is a problem, hang your tree upside-down from the ceiling and decorate your unique creation.

If you have a small balcony or porch outside of sliding glass doors, maybe a large tree could be decorated and kept standing outside for you and your guests to enjoy.

Use natural decorations and outdoor lights to trim the tree outside, and add a few trimmings for bird friends as well.

Beaded Christmas Decorations
Continued from page 13

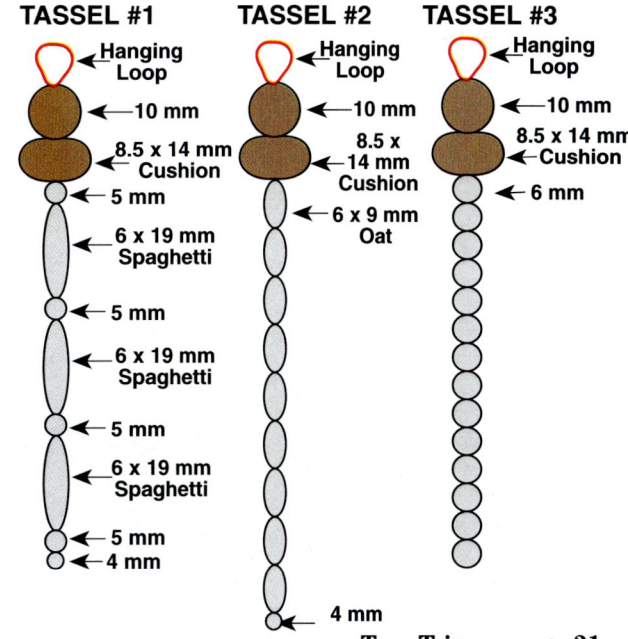

Angel Tree Topper

Designed by Jean Ashley

Finished Size:
Stands 15" high.

Materials:
- ❏ 3½" porcelain doll head and hands
- ❏ ½ yd. of royal blue with silver snowflakes fabric (or desired winter-print fabric)
- ❏ ½ yd. of silver lamé fabric
- ❏ 75" of white/iridescent feather boa
- ❏ 28" piece of ¼"-wide silver cording
- ❏ Two 2"-long crystal drops
- ❏ 40" of 1½"-wide silver mesh wire-edge ribbon
- ❏ 1½"-wide silver ribbon rose with leaves
- ❏ Small amount of quilt batting
- ❏ 15" high clear acrylic cone
- ❏ Pair of 15"-wide angel wings
- ❏ 12" chenille stem
- ❏ Sewing needle
- ❏ Blue and silver sewing threads
- ❏ Tape measure
- ❏ Scissors by Fiskars®
- ❏ Pinking shears by Fiskars®
- ❏ Crafty® Magic Melt® Oval Magic Pro Glue Gun by Adhesive Technologies, Inc.
- ❏ Crafty® Magic Melt® Glue Sticks by Adhesive Technologies, Inc.

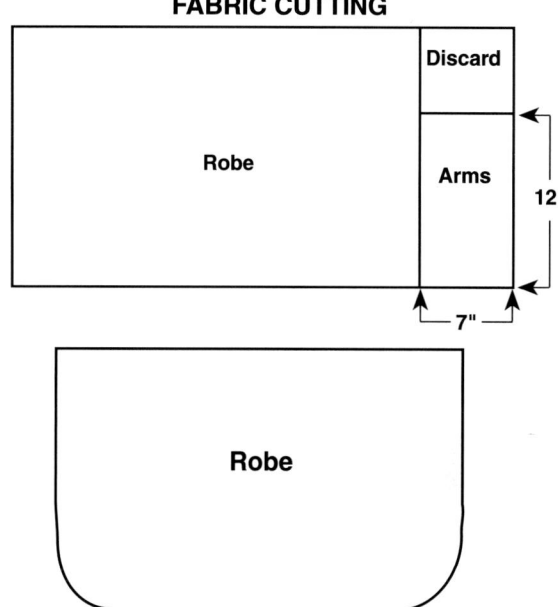

Instructions

1: For the **gown,** with the needle and thread, run a gathering stitch across one long end of the silver lamé fabric; pull the thread to gather tightly and fit around the top of the acrylic cone, secure the thread.

2: Glue the gathered edge of the gown around the top of the cone and glue the back edges of the gown together in several places.

3: For the **bottom edge** of the gown, turn the cone upside down and place a drop of glue on the inside of the cone about 1" from the bottom edge, fold the bottom edge of the gown 1" to the inside of the cone and press to adhere to the glue. Repeat this process around the cone, folding the bottom 1" of the gown to the inside of the cone, pleating it as necessary to glue in place. The gown should blouse at the bottom.

4: With the seam of the gown at the back, glue the head on top of the cone.

5: Cut the silver cord into one 10" piece and one 18" piece, set the 10" piece aside. Tie a small knot in each end of the 18" piece of cord. With the sewing needle and matching thread, sew a crystal drop to each knot. Fold the cord in half and glue the center of the cord to the lower front edge of the porcelain head; glue the silver ribbon rose over the folded center of the cord *(see photo)*.

6: For the **arms,** using the pinking shears, cut a 7" x 12" piece from the blue fabric *(see Fabric Cutting illustration)*. From the quilt batting, cut a 7" x 11" strip and lay it centered on top of the wrong side of the blue fabric.

7: Glue one of the porcelain hands to each end of the chenille stem; place the chenille stem in the center of the quilt batting and blue fabric. Roll the blue fabric around the batting and the chenille stem, forming a tube with the hands at each end; overlap the long ends of the blue fabric ½" and glue in place.

8: For the **cuffs,** gather the ends of the arm fabric around the wrist of each hand and glue the gathers to the hand. Cut a piece of silver ribbon to fit around the gathers and glue in place.

9: For the **robe,** using the pinking shears, cut around the entire outer edge of the robe fabric to prevent raveling, rounding the two bottom corners as you cut *(see Robe illustration)*.

10: With the sewing needle and matching thread, run a gathering stitch across the top straight edge of the robe fabric. Pulling the thread tightly to gather, fit the top edge of the robe around the shoulders of the porcelain head from one side of the rose, around to the opposite side of the rose, secure the thread. Glue the gathered edge of the robe to the head and body.

11: To **attach the arms** to the body, with the hands turned the appropriate direction and the seam of the arms facing toward the body, glue the center of the arms to the center back of the body.

12: Cut a 3"-long piece from one end of the feather boa and set it aside. Glue one end of the remaining length of boa to the center back of the head just below the hair; gluing

Continued on page 41

Crystal Prisms

Designed by Marilyn Shelton

Basic Materials:
- Jewelry pliers needed for each project:
    - Pointed-nose
    - Round-nose
    - Side cutter
- Scissors by Fiskars®
- Items listed for individual Prism
- Crafty® Magic Melt® Oval Magic Pro Glue Gun by Adhesive Technologies, Inc.
- Crafty® Magic Melt® Glue Sticks by Adhesive Technologies, Inc.

Basic Instructions

1: To **make an eye** in the end of an eye pin or a head pin, use the side cutters to cut off the point of the pin approximately $3/8$" above the last item. Use the pointed-nose pliers to bend the $3/8$" end in a 90-degree angle. Grasp the tip with the round-nose pliers and bend the $3/8$" section around the pliers so the end touches the wire to form a loop (see illustration).

2: To **join the prisms** together, insert a head pin in the appropriate hole of the first prism and make an eye in the end of the first head pin. Insert another head pin in the appropriate hole of the next prism, place the eye of the first head pin over the pointed end of the second head pin, make an eye in the end of the second head pin, enclosing the first eye.

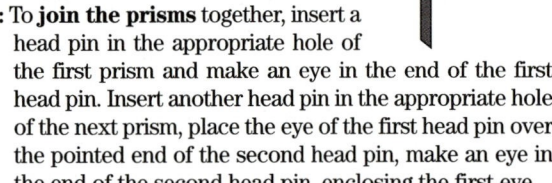

EYE
2: Bend into circle.
1: Bend at 90° angle.

Prism #1
(Shown at top right in photo)

Finished Size: 6" long.

Materials for One:
- 12" piece of $1/4$" Gold Morocco Cord by Offray
- $1½$" wide Metallic Gold Rose With Leaves by Offray
- 2" teardrop prism
- $5/8$" round prism
- 3 gold $7/8$" head pins
- Items listed in Basic Materials

Instructions

1: Fold the gold cord in half; holding the two ends together as one, tie an overhand knot (see illustration) about 1" from the ends of the cord. Fray the ends of the cord (see photo).
2: Join the teardrop prism to one side of the round prism (see Basic Instructions).
3: Insert a head pin in the remaining hole on the round prism, insert the pointed end of the head pin up into the knot on the cord, make an eye (see Basic Instructions) in the end of the head pin enclosing several strands of the cord to secure.
4: Glue the rose to the knot just above the round prism.

Prism #2
(Shown at center bottom in photo)

Finished Size: About $2¼$" long excluding ribbon.

Materials for One:
- 24" piece of $3/8$" Silver Wire Edge Mesh Ribbon by Offray
- $1½$" oval prism
- $5/8$" round prism
- 3 gold $7/8$" head pins
- Items listed in Basic Materials

Instructions

1: Cut a 7" piece of the silver ribbon, fold the ribbon in half, tie the ends in a knot.
2: Join the oval prism to the round prism (see Basic Instructions).
3: Insert a head pin in the remaining hole on the round prism, insert the pointed end of the head pin up into the knot on the ribbon, make an eye (see Basic Instructions) in the end of the head pin enclosing the ribbon to secure.
4: Tie the remaining length of silver ribbon in a 3"-wide double loop bow; glue the bow over the knot just above the round prism.

Prism #3
(Shown at bottom right in photo)

Finished Size: About $2¼$" long excluding ribbon.

Materials for One:
- 36" piece of $1/8$" Silver Quasar Woven Ribbon by Offray
- 2" teardrop prism
- $5/8$" round prism
- 3 gold $7/8$" head pins
- Silver Snowflake Charms by Creative Beginnings:
    - 2 small #9228
    - 2 medium #9227
    - 2 large #6039
- 6 Silver Jump Rings #2642 by Creative Beginnings
- Items listed in Basic Materials

Instructions

1: Cut a 7" piece of the silver ribbon, fold the ribbon in half, tie the ends in a knot forming a loop.

Continued on page 40

OVERHAND KNOT

Impressed Velvet Tree Skirt

Designed by Brenda Spitzer

Finished Size:
52"-diameter.

Materials:
- 3 yds. Bordeaux #5124 "Fidelio" Velvet by J.B. Martin
- 2¾ yds. of coordinating 44"-wide lining fabric
- 12" x 15" piece of $\frac{5}{32}$"-thick Handi Cork Natural Sheet Cork by Universal Cork, Inc. *(available at hardware stores)*
- Razor Knife #2607 by Fiskars®
- 3 pkgs. of size 5/0 Red Glass Seed Beads #5-022 by Creative Beginnings
- 36" piece of ½"-wide braided trim *(any color)*
- 24" square piece of tissue paper or craft paper
- Dark graphite paper
- Tracing paper
- Pencil
- Stylus
- Masking tape
- Double-sided tape
- Self-healing rotary cutting mat
- Scissors
- Straight pins
- Sewing needle and matching thread
- Steam iron
- Yardstick
- Small spray bottle of distilled water
- Sewing machine

Instructions

1: With the pencil, trace each of the Poinsettia Patterns on pages 39 and 40 onto tracing paper.

2: To make **cork templates,** place the graphite paper with the graphite side down on the cork sheet, place the traced patterns over the graphite paper and tape in place. Using the stylus or pencil, firmly trace over all pattern lines to transfer them to the cork. Remove the papers and tape.

3: Place the cork on the self-healing cutting mat. Using the razor knife, cut out around the outside pattern lines of each poinsettia.

4: To **cut the veining lines** on the petals, holding the knife blade at an angle and pulling the tip along one side of the line, cut a $\frac{1}{16}$"-deep groove in the cork along the

Continued on page 38

Impressed Velvet Tree Skirt
Continued from page 37

detail line. Then, angle the knife in the opposite direction and cut the other side of the line. Set the templates aside.

5: For the **Tree Skirt pattern**, using the yardstick and pencil, draw a pattern on the 24" piece of paper according to the Tree Skirt and Lining illustration and cut out.

6: Fold the velvet fabric in half lengthwise with right sides together. For each section of the Tree Skirt, place the fold line of the pattern even with the fold of the fabric, pin in place and cut out. Repeat for a total of four sections.

7: In the same manner, cut four sections from the lining fabric.

8: Fill the iron with distilled water and preheat to medium setting.

Note: The templates can be impressed on the velvet as shown in the photo by following the Suggested Template Placement diagram or as desired. Before impressing the velvet, experiment with the arrangement of the templates on the fabric, allowing ½" for seam allowances on each side of each fabric section and 1" at the bottom of each section. After determining the placement of the templates, place three or four small pieces of double-sided tape on the back of each template and secure it in the desired position with the detailed side up on the work surface.

9: Place one section of the velvet, right side down, on the templates and lightly spray the back of the velvet with the distilled water. To **impress the velvet,** place the iron on the fabric over one of the templates and press straight down with a steady pressure for about 15 seconds; lift the iron. Repeat this process until all of the templates have been impressed on the velvet. Continue pressing, repositioning the templates and fabric as needed to impress the section. Repeat for each fabric section. Let fabric dry.

10: Using needle and thread, randomly sew 10 to 15 beads to the center of each impressed flower.

11: To **assemble the Tree Skirt top,** place two velvet sections right sides together matching top edges and side edges; allowing ½" for seams, sew side edges together. Repeat with the remaining two sections. In the same manner, sew the assembled sections together along one side edge, leaving the remaining side edges unsewn for the Tree Skirt opening.

12: In the same manner, sew the four sections of the lining fabric together. Turn the bottom edge of the lining under ¼" and sew in place for a hem; set aside.

13: For the **Tree Skirt border,** cut enough 4"-wide bias strips *(see Bias Strips and Sewing diagrams)* from the remaining velvet to fit around the bottom edge of the Tree Skirt top plus 1" for side seam allowances; sew bias strips together. Place a straight pin on one long edge of the Tree Skirt border to designate this as the **top edge.**

14: To **impress the border,** secure the piece of braided trim in a straight line on the work surface with several small pieces of double-sided tape. Lay the border right side down on top of the braided trim with the trim 1¼" from the top edge of the fabric. Working in sections across the entire length of the border, spray lightly with distilled water and press as before to impress the fabric. Let fabric dry.

15: Fold each short end of the Tree Skirt border under ½" and sew in place. Matching the top edge of the border to the outer edge of the Tree Skirt top, pin the fabric pieces right sides together. Allowing ½" for seams and removing pins as you go, sew together.

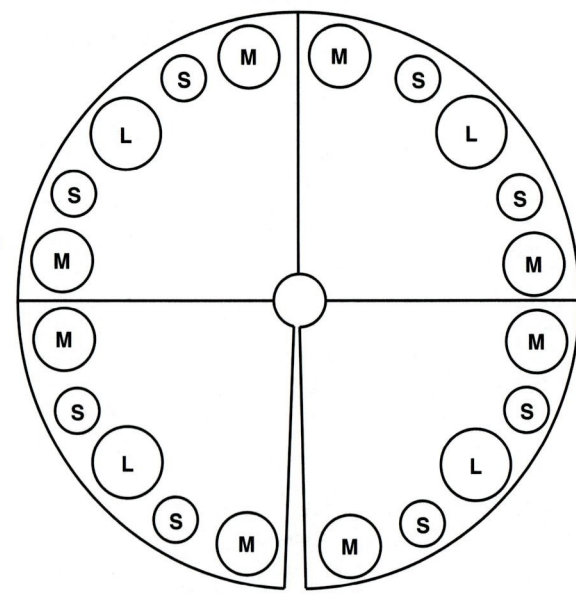

16: Fold the bottom edge of the border under ½" and sew in place for a hem.

17: Matching the top edge, seams and side edges, pin the Tree Skirt top and the lining right sides together. Allowing ½" for seams, sew around the side edges and the top of the Tree Skirt. Clip the curves and corners as needed to lay flat and turn right side out. From the lining side of the Tree Skirt, press the edges with a warm *(not hot)* iron.

18: Fold the bottom edge of the border under to meet the hemmed edge of the lining and pin in place. With sewing needle and thread, sew the bottom border edge to the hemmed edge of the lining.

Continued on page 40

SMALL POINSETTIA

MEDIUM POINSETTIA

Impressed Velvet Tree Skirt
Continued from page 39

LARGE POINSETTIA

Crystal Prisms
Continued from page 34

2: Join the teardrop prism to the round prism *(see Basic Instructions on page 34)*.

3: Insert a head pin in the remaining hole on the round prism, insert the pointed end of the head pin up into the knot on the ribbon, make an eye *(see Basic Instructions)* in the end of the head pin enclosing the ribbon to secure.

4: Tie the remaining length of silver ribbon in a 3"-wide multi-loop bow with 3"-long streamers; glue the bow over the knot just above the round prism. Cut one loop on each side of the bow to make two more streamers on each side.

5: To attach a small, a medium and a large snowflake to each side of the bow, use the pliers to spread the jump ring apart slightly, place a snowflake on the jump ring and insert one end of the jump ring through the end of one streamer; close the jump ring.

Prism #4
(Shown at left in photo)

Finished Size:
About $9\tfrac{1}{4}$" long excluding ribbon.

Materials for One:
❑ 36" piece of $\tfrac{1}{8}$" Gold Quasar Woven Ribbon by Offray

- ❏ 2" teardrop prism
- ❏ 1¼" octagonal prism
- ❏ 13 round ⅝" prisms
- ❏ 29 gold ⅞" head pins
- ❏ ½" Burgundy Satin Rose by Offray
- ❏ 1 yd. of ½"-wide Burgundy/Gold Wire Edge Mesh Ribbon by Offray
- ❏ Items listed in Basic Materials

Instructions

1: Cut a 10" piece of the gold ribbon, fold the ribbon in half and tie the ends in a knot, forming a loop.
2: Insert a head pin in one hole on the octagonal prism, insert the pointed end of the head pin up into the knot on the looped ribbon, make an eye in the end of the head pin *(see Basic Instructions on page 34)* enclosing the ribbon to secure.
3: Using twelve of the round prisms, join *(see Basic Instructions)* the prisms together to form a complete circle.
4: Insert a head pin in the remaining hole of the octa-gonal prism and join it to the circle of round prisms between any two prisms.
5: Join the remaining round prism to the center bottom of the circle of round prisms *(see photo)*; join the teardrop prism to the last round prism.
6: Cut an 8"-long piece from the gold ribbon. Lay this 8" piece of ribbon over the joining of the octagonal prism and the circle of round prisms *(see photo)*; with the remaining length of gold ribbon, tie a 3"-wide bow around this joining, enclosing the 8" piece of ribbon.
7: Glue the ribbon rose to the knot on the looped 10" piece of ribbon. Trim the ends of the ribbon in a "V" shape.

Prism #5
(Shown at center top in photo)

Finished Size:
About 2¼" long excluding ribbon.

Materials for One:
- ❏ 3 yds. of 1½" Gold Wire Edge Firefly Ribbon by Offray
- ❏ 2½" rectangular prism
- ❏ 2 round ⅝" prisms
- ❏ 1¼" octagonal prism
- ❏ 8 silver ⅞" head pins
- ❏ Items listed in Basic Materials

Instructions

1: Cut a 12" piece of the ribbon, fold the ribbon in half and tie the ends in a knot, forming a loop.
2: Join the octagonal prism to the rectangular prism *(see Basic Instructions on page 34)*.
3: Insert a head pin in the remaining hole on the octa-gonal prism, insert the pointed end of the head pin up into the knot on the looped ribbon, make an eye *(see Basic Instructions)* in the end of the head pin enclosing the ribbon to secure.
4: Join the two round prisms to the bottom of the rectangular prism *(see photo)*.
5: Cut a 14" piece from the ribbon. With the remaining length of ribbon, tie a 8"-wide multi-looped bow with 6" streamers, wrap the center of the bow with the 14" piece of ribbon and knot to secure. Glue the bow to the knot on the looped ribbon above the octagonal prism *(see photo)*. Trim the ends of the streamers at an angle.

❋ Symbols of Christmas – Poinsettia

In Mexican legend, a small boy knelt at the altar of his church on Christmas Eve. He had no gift for the Christ Child on his birthday, but his prayers were sincere and a miracle gave him the present that could be bought by no one; the first flower of the Holy Night sprang up at his feet in brilliant red homage to the holy birth.

Thus was born the flower we know as the poinsettia. Dr. Joel Roberts Poinsett brought the flower of the Holy Night back to his home in South Carolina. It became very popular as a Christmas plant and was named after him.

Angel Tree Topper
Continued from page 33

the boa to the very edge of the robe as you go, wrap the boa over one shoulder, down the front, around the bottom, up the opposite front side, over the shoulder and to the center back of the head *(see photo)*; cut off any excess.
13: At the back, glue the center of the wings to the center back of the arms *(see photo)*.
14: Run a 2"-long bead of glue down the center of the wings and place the 3" piece of the boa centered over the wings.
15: For the **halo,** tie the ends of the remaining 10" piece of silver cord in a square knot *(see illustration)*, forming a loop just slightly larger than the head. Trim the ends of the cord close to the knot and glue the knot centered on the back of the head above the wings.

Square Knot

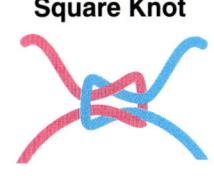

16: Drape the center of the silver ribbon across the back of the body, over each hand and down the front of the robe; secure the ribbon to the hands with a drop of glue on each cuff. ❋

Ribbon Rose Ornament

Designed by Denise Giles

Materials:
- Clear round 80 mm Crystal Globe #1105-97 by Darice®
- Ribbon by Offray:
    - 2 pieces each 36" long of 1½"-wide Comb. #18 Sorbet Ombre Wire Edge *(burgundy/green)*
    - 5 pieces each 7" long of 1½"-wide Comb. #21 Fern Ombre Wire Edge *(green)*
    - 12" of Gold Comb. #1 Metallic Chainette™
- Ribbon by Lion Ribbon Company, Inc,:
    - 2 pieces each 18" long of Dainty G ⅛"-wide Gold
    - 2 pieces each 18" long of Dainty G ⅛"-wide Nugget
- 1" square of floral foam
- Small amount of moss
- 7 pieces of floral wire each 3" long
- Scissors
- Pencil
- Kid's Choice Glue!™ by Beacon™ or craft glue

Instructions

1: For each **gathered ribbon rose** *(make 2)*, tie a small knot in one end of one piece of burgundy/green ribbon to secure the wires. On the opposite end, while firmly holding the wire on the **green** side, push the ribbon down the wire to gather the entire length of the ribbon forming soft ruffles along the burgundy side of the ribbon.

2: Hold the knot in one hand and tightly wrap the gathered edge around the knot two times to form the center of the rose, continue loosely wrapping the gathered ribbon around the knot to form the outer petals of the rose. When all of the ribbon has been wrapped around the knot, secure the rose by tightly wrapping the long wire around the knot several times. Cut off the excess wire.

3: For each **leaf** *(make 5)*, fold one 7" piece of green ribbon in half and gently pull both of the wires on the lighter green side of the ribbon to gather *(see step 1 on Gathered Leaf illustration)*; open up the side of the ribbon that has not been gathered to shape the leaf *(see step 2 on illustration)*. To secure the leaf, tightly wrap one end of a 3" piece of floral wire around the bottom edge of the leaf, leaving a 1" end on the wire *(see step 3 on illustration)*. Trim the ribbon wire ends.

4: Leaving a 1" end, wrap one 3" piece of floral wire around the bottom of each rose.

5: To **assemble the roses and leaves,** insert the wire from one rose into one side of the floral foam, insert the wire from the remaining rose on the opposite side of the floral foam. In the same manner, attach each leaf evenly spaced around the sides of the floral foam between the two roses.

6: To fill in any gaps between the roses or the leaves, break off a small piece of moss and glue it in place as desired.

7: Open up the crystal globe and place the roses inside. Run a bead of glue around the inner edge on one half of the globe, reassemble the globe and wipe away any excess glue; let dry.

8: Cut a piece of the gold ribbon to fit around the seam of the globe and glue in place; let dry. With the remaining gold ribbon, fold a 3"-wide double-looped bow and glue it to one side of the globe hanger; let dry. Wrap the streamers of the bow around a pencil to curl the ends.

9: Cut the nugget ribbon in half and fold each piece of the ribbon into a 3"-wide single-looped bow. Glue one bow to each side of the ornament hanger; let dry. Wrap each of the gold streamers around a pencil to curl the ends.

10: For the **hanger,** thread one end of the gold chainette through the hole in the globe hanger, tie the ends together to form a loop.

GATHERED LEAF

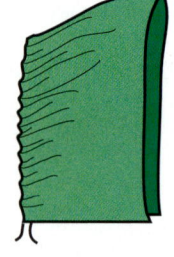

1: Gather ribbon on wire at center edge.

2: Separate sides at fold and shape into a Leaf.

3: Wrap ends tightly with wire.

CHAPTER TWO
Entertaining Delights

From elaborate family feasts to a cozy gathering for friends, you can enjoy an entire holiday season of delicious dining, and express the spirit of the season through your holiday decor!

Ornament Place Cards

Designed by Blanche Lind

Finished Sizes:
Each ornament is about 5" tall.

Ruth

Materials:
- 2½" gold satin ball ornament
- 4" square piece of burgundy felt and green felt
- 5 small gold rhinestones
- 10 mm gold bell cap
- 12" piece of ¼"-wide Christmas-print bias tape
- 10" piece of green 18-gauge wire
- Red and green calligraphy pens
- 3" × 5" unruled index card
- Tracing paper and pencil
- Decorative scissors
- Straight-edge scissors
- Needle-nose pliers
- Hot glue gun and glue sticks

Instructions
1. Remove the plastic hanger from the satin ball. Glue the open end of the bell cap to the top of the ball, covering the hanger hole.
2. Trace the Leaf and the Petal patterns onto tracing paper and cut out. With straight-edge scissors, cut three Leaves from the green felt; cut six Small Petals and six Large Petals from the burgundy felt.

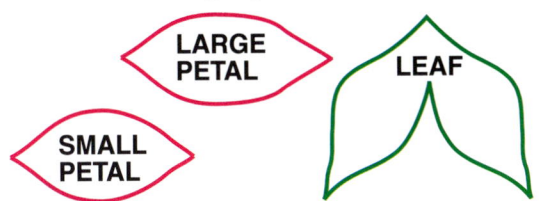

3. To glue each petal in place, apply a small drop of glue to one tip of the petal. With glued tips meeting at the center and leaving the other tips loose, glue the six Large Petals evenly spaced in a circle on one side of the ball. In the same manner, glue the six Small Petals on top centered between the Large Petals (see photo).
4. Glue three Leaves evenly spaced around the flower, tucking the center tips of the Leaves underneath the loose edges of the Petals (see photo).
5. Glue the five gold rhinestones at the center of the Small Petals.
6. For the **stand**, cut a ¼" × 6" strip from the index card. Cut a 6" piece of bias tape. Wrap the bias tape around the card strip, covering both sides completely; glue in place. With the raw edges of the bias tape on the inside, shape the strip into a circle with the ends overlapping ¼"; glue to secure.
7. Glue the stand to the bottom of the ball.
8. For the **Wire Card Holder**, gently bend the 18-gauge wire in a loop; with pliers, wrap one end of the wire in a spiral around the other end of the wire several times (see Wire Card Holder illustration). Bend the looped end of the wire down toward the center (see dotted line on illustration).
9. Place a drop of glue on the straight end of the Holder and insert the Holder through the top of the bell cap and into the ball.
10. For the **Place Card**, using decorative scissors, cut a 1¼" × 2¼" piece from the index card. With calligraphy pens, outline the edges of the Card and write the name in the center of the Card.
11. Decorate the Card as desired. Place the Card in the Holder (see photo).

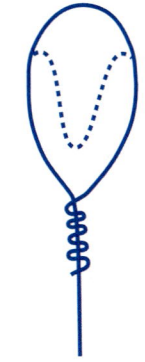

WIRE CARD HOLDER

Nicole

Materials:
- 2½" white satin ball ornament
- 2 yds. of gold 3 mm strung beads
- 4½' of gold 10 mm strung beads
- 15" piece of gold star garland
- 8" piece of silver 18-gauge wire
- Gold spray glitter
- Gold calligraphy pen
- 3" × 5" unruled index card
- Decorative scissors
- Straight-edge scissors
- Needle-nose pliers
- Hot glue gun and glue sticks

Instructions
1. Remove the plastic hanger from the satin ball.
2. Cut one 8" strand and ten 4" strands from the 3 mm strung beads.
3. Wrap the 8" strand of strung beads around the ball beginning and ending at the hole made by the plastic hanger (see photo); secure with a drop of glue at each end and at the bottom of ball.
4. Glue five 4" strands evenly spaced around each half of the ball, beginning at the hole and ending at the center bottom (see photo).
5. For the **stand**, glue the ends of the 10 mm strung beads together to form a circle. Glue the stand to the bottom of the ball.
6. With the pliers, twist the star garland in a spiral, leaving 2" of one end straight. Place a small drop of glue on the tip of the straight end and insert it into the hole at the top of the ball. Gently pull the garland to spread the spiral (see photo).
7. Lightly spray the entire ball with gold glitter.
8. For the **Spiral Card Holder**, with pliers, twist one end of

Continued on page 55

Bow and Holly
Mosaic Tray

Designed by Phyllis Dobbs

Finished Size:
Tray is 2" x 11" x 15".

Materials:
- 2" x 11" x 15" Wood Serving Tray #3580 by Walnut Hollow
- Make-it Mosaics™ Bag o' Chips by Plaid®:
    - 4 bags of White #67129
    - 2 bags of Red #67137
    - 1 bag of Green #67140
- Make-it Mosaics™ Adhesive by Plaid® (glue)
- Make-it Mosaics™ Tile Nipper by Plaid®
- Make-it Mosaics™ White Sanded Tile Grout by Plaid®
- Aleene's™ Premium-Coat™ Holiday Green #OC181 Acrylic Paint by Duncan Enterprises
- Aleene's™ Premium-Coat™ Enhancer Satin Varnish #EN102-8 by Duncan Enterprises
- Safety glasses
- Hammer
- Old thick towel
- Rags or sponge
- 2 sheets graphite transfer paper
- 2 sheets tracing paper
- Transparent tape
- Pencil
- Craft stick
- Rubber spatula
- Small paintbrush

Instructions

1: To transfer the bow and holly patterns *(see lines behind text on page 63)* to the tray, place two sheets of tracing paper side-by-side and tape them together. Trace the red lines of the bow pattern centered at the top of the two pieces of tracing paper. Trace the purple lines of the streamer pattern on the right side of the bow matching the open end of the streamer with the dotted lines on the bow. Turn the tracing paper over and trace the purple lines of the streamer pattern onto the opposite side of the bow matching the dotted lines. Using the photo as a guide, randomly trace the green lines of the holly leaf pattern to make three holly leaves below the bow, leaving room between the leaves to place four red tile chips for berries.

2: Tape the two pieces of graphite paper together the same as the tracing paper. Place the graphite paper face down in the center of the tray; position the traced bow and leaf pattern over the graphite paper and tape in place. Trace over the pattern lines, pressing firmly to transfer the design. Remove the tape and papers.

Caution: *Always wear safety glasses when breaking or*

Continued on page 63

Entertaining Delights ~ page 49

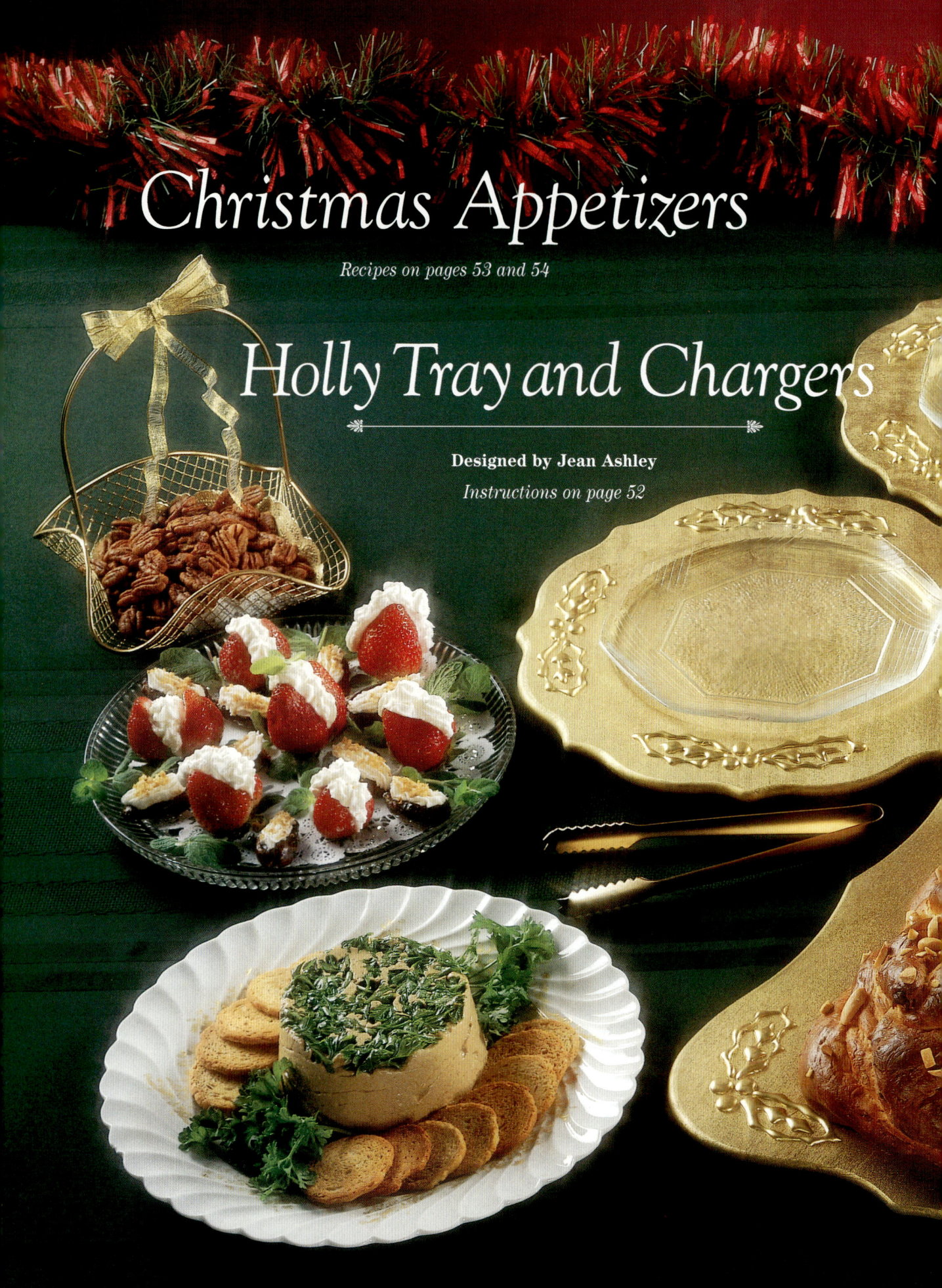

Christmas Appetizers

Recipes on pages 53 and 54

Holly Tray and Chargers

Designed by Jean Ashley

Instructions on page 52

Frozen Holiday Ice Bucket

Designed by Minette Collins Smith

Instructions on page 53

Entertaining Delights ~ page 51

Holly Tray and Chargers
Photo on pages 50 and 51

Finished Sizes:
Chargers are 11½" across; Tray is 12" x 15".

Materials:
- Unpainted Wooden Items by Walnut Hollow:
    Two 11½"-diameter Chippendale Plates
        #3553 *(for Chargers)*
    12" x 15" Chippendale Tray #3556
- Gold Metallic #1706 Spray Paint by Krylon®
- Black felt:
    2 pieces each 10" square for Chargers
    11" x 15" piece for Tray
- Sandpaper
- Tack cloth or damp rag
- Tracing paper
- Graphite paper
- Pencil
- Craft glue
- Crafty® Magic Melt® Oval Magic Pro Glue Gun by Adhesive Technologies, Inc.
- Crafty® Magic Melt® Glue Sticks by Adhesive Technologies, Inc.

Preparation
With sandpaper, lightly sand uneven edges or rough surfaces from the Tray and Chargers; wipe with tack cloth or damp rag to remove sanding dust.

Tray
1: To transfer the holly design to the Tray, trace the Tray Pattern onto tracing paper; place the graphite paper with graphite-side down, centered on one corner of the Tray *(see photo)*; place the traced design over the graphite paper and firmly trace the design. Repeat on each corner of the Tray.
2: Using the hot glue gun, outline each of the leaves and fill in each berry outline with hot glue. Let dry.
3: With gold, paint the top, bottom and outer edges of the Tray. Let dry. Apply a second coat if needed for complete coverage.
4: Spread a thin layer of craft glue over the bottom of the Tray. Lay the appropriate piece of felt over the glued area and smooth it out. Let dry. Trim excess felt from the edges.

Chargers
1: For each Charger, to transfer the design, trace the Charger Pattern onto tracing paper; with graphite-side down, place the graphite paper over the outer rim of the Charger, place the traced design over the graphite paper and firmly trace the design; repeat four times evenly spaced around the Charger *(see photo)*.
2: Using the hot glue gun, outline each of the leaves and fill in each berry outline with hot glue. Let dry.
3: With gold, paint the top, bottom and outer edges of the Charger. Let dry. Apply a second coat if needed for complete coverage.
4: Spread a thin layer of craft glue over the bottom of the Charger. Lay the appropriate piece of felt over the glued area and smooth it out. Let dry. Trim excess felt from the edges.

❋ Symbols of Christmas – Holly

Holly is a familiar green shrub, usually having red berries and dark glossy green leaves with thorny tips and flourishes in almost every kind of soil. The bright colors of the holly made it a natural symbol of rebirth and life in the winter whiteness of northern Europe. In late December, the Teutonic peoples traditionally placed holly and other evergreens around the interior of dwellings to ward off winter bad weather and unwanted spirits.

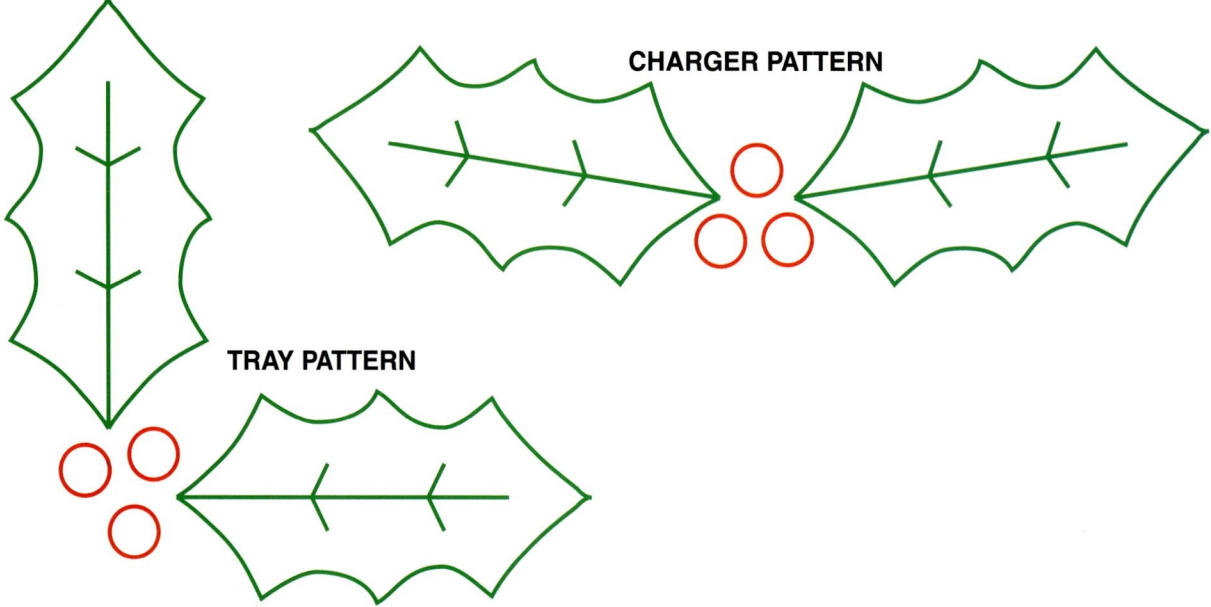

TRAY PATTERN

CHARGER PATTERN

Frozen Holiday Ice Bucket

Photo on pages 50 and 51

Finished Size:
Size of container chosen.

Materials for One:
- 5- or 6-quart plastic utility bucket
- Large paper cup or other paper container large enough for a wine bottle to fit inside
- Gravel or small rocks to fill paper container
- Small real or artificial poinsettias
- Real or artificial holly leaves with red berries
- Tray or plate with raised rim to hold water from melting ice

Instructions

1: Fill the paper container with gravel.
2: Place the paper container in the center of the plastic bucket.
3: Arranging the flowers and greenery to be attractive from the outside, place the poinsettias and holly in the bucket around the paper container.
4: Fill the bucket with water to 1" below the top of the paper container or bucket — whichever is lower. Place the bucket in the freezer until the water is frozen solid.
5: To unmold the Frozen Ice Bucket, remove the gravel from the paper container; fill the container with hot water and quickly remove the container as soon as it will lift out.
6: To loosen the ice from the plastic bucket, place the bucket in a sink filled with warm water; as soon as the ice melts enough to release it, lift the Frozen Ice Bucket out of the plastic bucket. Return the Frozen Ice Bucket to the freezer until ready to use.
7: To use, place the Frozen Ice Bucket on the tray or plate to catch the water as it melts; place a bottle of wine or other holiday drink in the cavity formed by the paper container.

Christmas Appetizer Recipes

Photo on pages 50 and 51

by Linda Moll Smith

NOEL BRAID
This impressive loaf is derived from traditional German and Bohemian Christmas breads.

½ cup butter
1 cup sugar
2 cakes live yeast
2 cups scalded milk
2 egg yolks, reserving whites
2 whole eggs
1 teaspoon nutmeg
1 tablespoon salt
½ pound golden raisins OR ½ pound mixed citron
¼ pound blanched, slivered almonds, reserving a few for garnish
6 cups unbleached or all-purpose flour

Glaze:
2 egg whites
2 tablespoons cold water
2 tablespoons butter, melted
Small amount of blanched, slivered almonds for garnish

Scald the milk and cool to lukewarm.

To be sure the yeast is active, crumble the yeast into a small bowl and add 1 teaspoon of the sugar and ¼ cup of the warm milk. Let stand for five minutes; it should become slightly foamy — if not, use other yeast.

Cream the remaining sugar with the butter, add the egg yolks and eggs one at a time, beating thoroughly after each addition.

Add nutmeg, salt, raisins and all but a small amount of the almonds (reserved for garnish), stir in enough flour to make a soft dough that can be handled.

Turn the dough out on a lightly floured surface and knead until smooth and elastic. Place in a lightly greased bowl, cover and let rise until doubled (about 1½ hours).

Punch down dough and knead a few times, then with a sharp knife, divide the dough into 9 parts: 4 large, 3 medium and 2 small. Roll each part into a rope-like strand.

Braid the 4 large strands together and place on a lightly greased baking sheet.

Braid the 3 medium strands together and place on top of the four-strand braid.

Twist together the 2 small strands and center on top of the other braids.

Allow to rise until doubled (about 45 minutes to an hour).

Check on the loaf after about 20 minutes; if the braids are beginning to shift as they rise, secure them with bamboo skewers placed in the dough at angles and allow to continue rising.

Preheat oven to 350° while loaf is rising.

Beat 2 egg whites with 2 tablespoons cold water just until blended; brush on all surfaces of the loaf. Sprinkle with the reserved almonds.

Bake for 45 minutes to an hour or until well-browned. If after 20 minutes, the loaf is browning too quickly, cover loosely with an aluminum foil tent.

When done, brush with melted butter while the loaf is still warm. Remove bamboo skewers, if used. Let cool.

To serve: Slice across the braids at an angle. Offer with butter.

Continued on page 54

Christmas Appetizer Recipes
Continued from page 53

MOROCCAN MEATBALLS

1 pound ground meat (half beef and half lamb is nice)
3 teaspoons cumin, divided
1 teaspoon ground ginger
¼ teaspoon ground cloves
¼ teaspoon cinnamon
1 teaspoon nutmeg, divided
1 teaspoon black pepper, divided
½ teaspoon cayenne pepper
1¼ cup sour cream, divided
1 tablespoon lemon juice
Grape tomatoes, capers and cocktail picks for garnish

Preheat oven to 350°.
Combine meat, 2 teaspoons cumin, ginger, cloves, cinnamon, ½ teaspoon nutmeg, ½ teaspoon black pepper, cayenne and ¼ cup sour cream in bowl; mix together well.
Form mixture into 1-inch balls.
Bake on a jelly roll pan at 350° for 6–8 minutes, or until browned, turning if desired.
Remove meatballs from the pan and place in a skillet.
In a small bowl, blend lemon juice, remaining cumin, nutmeg, pepper and sour cream until mixed.
Pour over meatballs, cover and simmer over low heat for 15 to 20 minutes.
Keep warm in a chafing dish and serve with cocktail picks, topped with grape tomatoes and capers. Makes about 30 meatballs.

BOURBON STREET CHICKEN LIVER PATE

½ pound chicken livers
3 tablespoons butter
2 tablespoons melted butter
4 hard-boiled eggs, chopped
1 small onion, finely chopped
2 tablespoons fresh parsley, minced
Tabasco and Worcestershire sauces
4–5 tablespoons bourbon, divided

Soak chicken livers in cold salted water or cold milk for an hour in the refrigerator. Rinse and drain well.
Broil livers gently in butter and 2 tablespoons bourbon, cooking them until done, but still soft.
Place eggs, butter and onion in blender and blend well. Add chicken livers and blend until creamy.
Add Tabasco and Worcestershire sauces to taste.
Pour into desired container and chill.
To serve: Unmold onto a serving plate; pour remaining bourbon over and ignite. Serve with melba rounds.

STRAWBERRIES & DATES DELIGHT

8 oz. package of cream cheese, softened
⅓ cup sugar
1 cup sour cream
2 teaspoons vanilla
8 oz. container of frozen whipped topping, thawed
24 large ripe strawberries, washed and blotted dry
24 pitted ripe dates
¼ cup finely crumbled ginger snap cookies

Beat cream cheese until smooth; gradually blend in sugar a small amount at a time.
Blend in sour cream and vanilla.
Fold in whipped topping, blending well.
Cross-slice strawberries from the ends almost through to the stems.
Slice dates down the middle, and plump to open.
Spoon cream cheese filling into a cake icing bag and pipe into each piece of fruit.
Sprinkle with ginger snap crumbs.
Chill until ready to serve.

BLAZING GLAZED NUTS

3 tablespoons cider vinegar
2 tablespoons brown or white sugar
½ teaspoon cayenne pepper (more if you dare!)
2 cups pecans
1 teaspoon butter, melted
½ teaspoon garlic salt

Preheat oven to 250°.
Mix vinegar, sugar and cayenne pepper in a quart jar. Add pecans and place lid on the jar; shake to coat pecans thoroughly.
Place pecans on a baking sheet and toast at 250° until lightly browned, stirring frequently.
Add butter and salt and toss to coat nuts.
Continue baking until toasted.
Let cool. Refrigerate in an airtight container to keep them crisp.

Ornament Place Cards
Continued from page 47

the 18-gauge wire in a spiral *(see Spiral Card Holder illustration)*, leaving opposite end straight. Place a drop of glue on the tip of the straight end of the wire and insert it into the top of ball.

9: For the **Place Card,** using decorative scissors, cut a $1\frac{1}{4}" \times 2\frac{1}{4}"$ piece from the index card. With the calligraphy pen, outline the edges of the card and write the name in the center of the card.

10: Decorate the card as desired. Place the card in the Holder *(see photo)*.

SPIRAL CARD HOLDER

Sharon
Materials:
- ❑ $2\frac{1}{2}"$ white satin ball ornament
- ❑ 400 white 3 mm pearls *(loose)*
- ❑ Gold glitter
- ❑ 12" piece of gold striped wire-edge ribbon
- ❑ 9" piece of copper 18-gauge wire
- ❑ $4\frac{1}{2}"$ strand of gold 10 mm beads
- ❑ 1" gold flat button
- ❑ 4" piece of florist wire
- ❑ Gold calligraphy pen
- ❑ 3" × 5" unruled index card
- ❑ Decorative scissors
- ❑ Straight-edge scissors
- ❑ Needle-nose pliers
- ❑ Hot glue gun and glue sticks
- ❑ Craft glue

Instructions

1: Remove the plastic hanger from the satin ball.

2: For the **Spiral Card Holder,** with pliers, twist one end of the 18-gauge wire in a spiral *(see Spiral Card Holder illustration)*, leaving opposite end straight. Place a drop of hot glue on the tip of the straight end of the wire and insert it into the top of the ball. Let dry.

3: Holding the ball by the Card Holder, swirl craft glue in a random circular design around the entire surface of the ball; sprinkle glitter over the glue; let dry. Shake off excess glitter.

4: In each open area of the ball, spread craft glue between the lines of glitter, sprinkle loose pearls on the glue and gently pat the pearls into the glue. Let dry.

5: Fold the ribbon into a $3\frac{1}{2}"$-wide bow; wrap the center with florist wire. Apply hot glue to the ends of the wire and insert them into the top of the ball next to the Card Holder.

6: Glue the flat button to the bottom of the ball with hot glue.

7: For the **stand,** glue the ends of the 10 mm strung beads together to form a circle. Place the stand around the button at the bottom of the ball.

8: For the **Place Card,** using decorative scissors, cut a $1\frac{1}{4}" \times 2\frac{1}{4}"$ piece from the index card. With the calligraphy pen, outline the edges of the card and write the name in the center of the card.

9: Decorate the card as desired. Place the card in the Holder *(see photo)*.

Cindy
Materials:
- ❑ $2\frac{1}{2}"$ white satin ball ornament
- ❑ 8 red round jewels
- ❑ 16" piece of red sequin rickrack
- ❑ 4 red square jewels
- ❑ 10 mm gold bell cap
- ❑ 8" piece of red 18-gauge wire
- ❑ Red calligraphy pen
- ❑ 3" × 5" unruled index card
- ❑ Decorative scissors
- ❑ Straight-edge scissors
- ❑ Needle-nose pliers
- ❑ Hot glue gun and glue sticks

Instructions

1: Remove the plastic hanger from the satin ball.

2: Cut two pieces of rickrack each 8" long. Beginning and ending at the hanger hole, gluing in place as you go, wrap one piece around the ball *(see photo)*.

3: In the same manner, wrap the remaining 8" piece of rickrack around the ball centered between the first piece *(see photo)*.

4: Glue one square jewel and two round jewels in each section of the ball *(see photo)*.

5: Glue the open end of the bell cap to the top of the ball, covering the hanger hole and the ends of the rickrack.

6: For the **stand,** cut a $\frac{1}{4}" \times 6"$ strip from the index card. Shape the strip into a circle with the ends overlapping $\frac{1}{4}"$, glue to secure.

7: Cut a strip of rickrack to fit around the outside of the stand, plus $\frac{1}{2}"$. Glue the rickrack around the outside of the stand, overlapping the ends.

8: For the **Spiral Card Holder,** with pliers, twist one end of the 18-gauge wire in a spiral *(see Spiral Card Holder illustration)*, leaving opposite end straight. Place a drop of glue on the tip of the straight end of the wire and insert it in the ball.

9: For the **Place Card,** using decorative scissors, cut a $1\frac{1}{4}" \times 2\frac{1}{4}"$ piece from the index card. With the calligraphy pen, outline the edges of the card and write the name in the center of the card.

10: Decorate the card as desired. Place the card in the Holder *(see photo)*. ❦

Christmas Card Tea Tray and Coaster

Designed by Marilyn Shelton

Finished Sizes:
   Tray is 1⅝" × 10" × 13", plus handles. Coaster is 6" across.

Materials:
- Medium Tea Tray #80061 by Sudberry House, Inc.
- Coaster #15801 by Sudberry House, Inc.
- Package of Keep A Memory™ Mounting Adhesive Sheets #3821 by Therm O Web
- Keep A Memory™ Sticky Dots Adhesive #4051 by Therm O Web
- Felt (*optional – if not provided by Tray and Coaster manufacturer*):
    9" × 12" rectangular
    5" circle
- Several old Christmas cards
- Glass cleaner
- Paper towels
- Scissors

Tea Tray

1: Carefully bend back the framer points on the back of the Tea Tray and remove the cardboard insert and the mounting board.
2: Trim Christmas cards to the desired shape and size.
3: Decide how best to arrange the cards on the mounting board, placing larger cards at the back and layering and overlapping the cards to blend the edges.
4: Following the manufacturer's instructions, apply one adhesive sheet centered on the top of the mounting board. Remove the release paper from the adhesive.
5: Position the larger background cards as desired on mounting board and firmly press in place.
6: Following the manufacturer's instructions, use the sticky dots adhesive to layer smaller cards and accent pieces as desired.
7: With glass cleaner and paper towels, clean both sides of the glass inside the tray to remove fingerprints.
8: Turn the tray upside down and place the mounting board facedown in the tray; lay the cardboard insert on top of the mounting board. Carefully bend the framer points back down to secure the mounting board.
9: Adhere the 9" x 12" felt rectangle to the center bottom of the tray; firmly press in place to secure.

Coaster

1: Remove the glass dish and mounting board from the wooden base of the coaster.
2: Choose a Christmas card large enough to cover the mounting board; trim the card to fit.
3: Cut a piece from one mounting adhesive sheet to cover the mounting board. Following the manufacturer's instructions, apply the adhesive sheet to the mounting board.
4: Remove the release paper from the adhesive sheet; lay the card in place and press firmly.
5: Place the mounting board face up in the base of the coaster, replace the glass dish.
6: Adhere the 5" circle of felt to the center bottom of the coaster.

Entertaining Delights ~ page 57

Christmas Dinner

Recipes on pages 62 and 63

Entertaining Delights ~ page 58

Wired Poinsettia Table Set

Photo on pages 58 & 59

Materials:
- ❑ Artistic Wire by Helwig Industries or 22-gauge wire:
    - Natural #22-10 *(copper)*
    - Magenta #22-09 *(red)*
    - Aqua #22-01 *(green)*
- ❑ Wire Working Jewelry Tools by Helwig Industries:
    - WigJig Olympus *(jig)*
    - 28 Pegs
- ❑ 2 clear glass candlesticks
- ❑ Bamboo skewer *(or similar item)*
- ❑ Round pencil or pen
- ❑ Wire Cutters by Fiskars®

Basic Instructions *(use with instructions for individual item)*

1: Following the appropriate Grid Pattern, place pegs in the proper holes of the jig as indicated by the brown dots on each pattern.
2: Before wrapping the wire, anchor the end of the wire by folding about 1½" around to the back of the jig. This is the **tie wire.**
3: When wrapping the wire around the pegs, pull the wire snug against the peg to get the proper shape *(diagrams shown loose for better detail)*.
4: Following the colored lines on the appropriate Wrap Pattern, begin at the starting point indicated on the Pattern and wrap the wire across the jig, going under peg 1, up and over peg 2 *(blue line)*.
5: Wrap wire over the top of peg 3, down and around peg 1 *(pink line)*.
6: Wrap wire up and over peg 3, across and over peg 4 *(lt. green line)*.
7: Wrap wire down and around peg 1, up and over peg 2, under peg 5, over peg 6, between pegs 5 and 7, down and around peg 3 *(dk. green line)*.
8: Wrap wire up and over peg 6, down between pegs 5 and 7, over peg 4, bring wire down to peg 1 *(red line)*.
9: After wrapping the first petal or leaf, turn the jig counter-clockwise and repeat the wrapping process on the next set of pegs to the right *(see blue line)*; continue until all pegs have been used.
10: When the last petal or leaf is completed, cut the wire leaving about ½".
11: To **remove the wire from the jig,** gently slide the wire up and off of the pegs. The design will bow upward slightly and will seem to come apart, but it will retain the basic shape.
12: Wrap the ½" end of wire around the base of the last petal or leaf made.

Table Decoration *(make 2)*

Petals

1: For **one set of Petals,** place pegs as shown on the Large Grid Pattern. Using red wire, wrap four Petals as shown on the Large Flower Wrap Pattern.
2: Gently remove the wire from the pegs and set it aside.
3: Repeat steps 1 and 2 to make another set of Petals.
4: To **join the two sets,** place the first set centered on top of the second set, bowed sides up. Rotate the first set to fill in spaces between the second set.
5: To **secure the design,** wrap one tie wire around the base of each Petal all around; wrap the remaining tie wire in the opposite direction.

Leaves

1: For **one set of Leaves,** place pegs as shown on the Large Grid Pattern. Using green wire, wrap four Leaves as shown on the Large Flower Wrap Pattern.
2: Gently remove the wire from the pegs and set it aside.
3: Repeat steps 1 and 2 to make another set of Leaves.
4: To **join the two sets,** place the first set centered on top of the second set, bowed sides up. Rotate the first set to fill in spaces between the second set.
5: Gently turn the Leaves over on the work surface with

LARGE GRID PATTERN

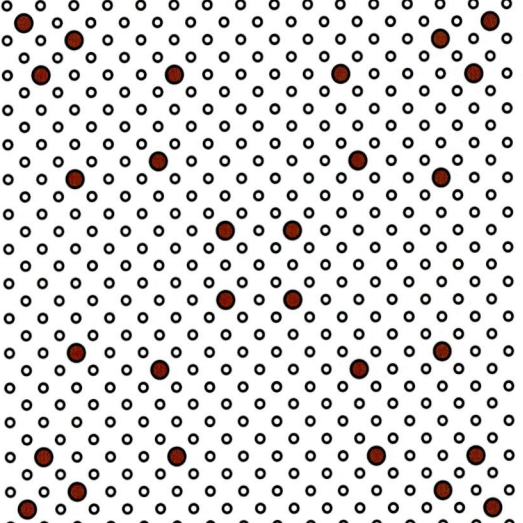

LARGE FLOWER WRAP

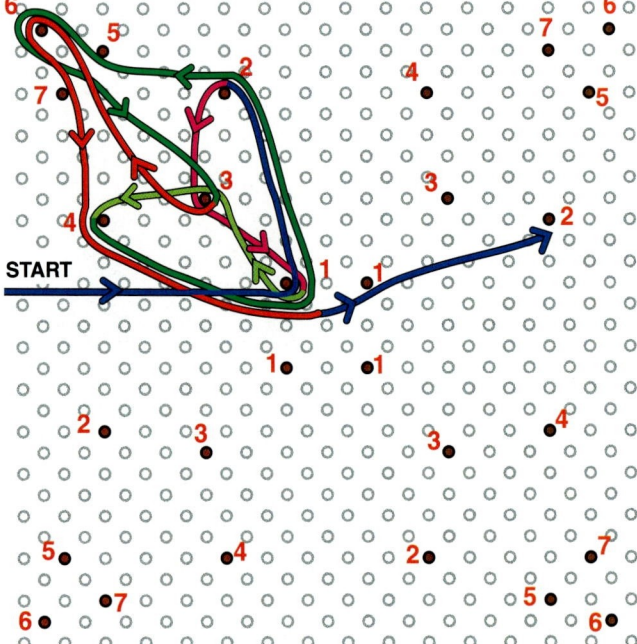

✺ Spice Up the Holidays

Combine in a pan:
  Peeling of 2 oranges
  3 cinnamon sticks
  12 whole clove
  2 cups of water

Simmer on the back burner, adding water when needed, to fill the whole house with a continuous Christmas aroma.

Or sprinkle ground cinnamon on the burners of an electric stove. When they're turned on, the incense of cinnamon fills the air.

bowed sides down. Place the Petals, bowed sides up, centered on top of the Leaves.

6: To **secure the design,** working around the base of the Leaves and the Petals at the same time, wrap the two tie wires from the Leaves in the same manner as step 5 of the Petal set.

Stamens

1: Using a bamboo skewer and copper wire, wrap the wire repeatedly around the skewer, pushing the loops together as you work so it looks like a spring, until you have a coil about 8" long.
2: Slide the coil off the skewer. With the wire cutters, cut the coil into eight segments each about 1" long. Gently pull the center of each coil segment apart slightly.
3: Working from the back of the flower, between the Leaves and Petals, fold the center of one coil segment around the tie wire, twist to secure. Bend half of each coil segment toward the center of the flower and the other half of the segment pointing upward.

Finishing

1: Gently cup the Petals in both hands and bend them upward slightly *(see photo)*.
2: In the same manner, gently bend the Leaves down.

Candleholder *(make 2)*

1: For **Petals,** work steps 1–4 of Table Decoration Petals.
2: For **Leaves,** work steps 1–4 of the Table Decoration Leaves.
3: To **secure the design,** spread the center of the Petals and Leaves apart to fit over the candlesticks; wrap the tie wires around the base of each Petal and Leaf as instructed in step 5 of the Table Decoration Petals.
4: For **Stamens,** work steps 1–3 of Table Decoration Stamens.
5: Work Table Decoration Finishing.

Napkin Ring *(make 2)*

1: For **Petals,** using the Small Grid Pattern for peg placement and the Small Flower Wrap Pattern, work steps 1–5 of the Table Decoration Petals.
2: For **Leaves,** using the Small Grid Pattern and Small Flower Wrap Pattern, follow steps 1–5 of the Table Decoration Leaves.
3: For **Stamens,** work step 1 of the Table Decoration Stamens to make a 7"-long coil.
4: Cut the coil into seven segments each 1" long. Gently pull apart at the center of each segment.
5: Work step 3 of the Table Decoration Stamens.
6: Work Table Decoration Finishing.
7: For the **ring,** wrap the green wire repeatedly around a pen or pencil creating a continuous coil about 5" long. Gently remove the coil.
8: Twist one end of the coil around the tie wire on the back of the assembled flower. Twist the remaining coil end around the first coil end to interlock the two ends and form a circle. ✺

SMALL GRID PATTERN

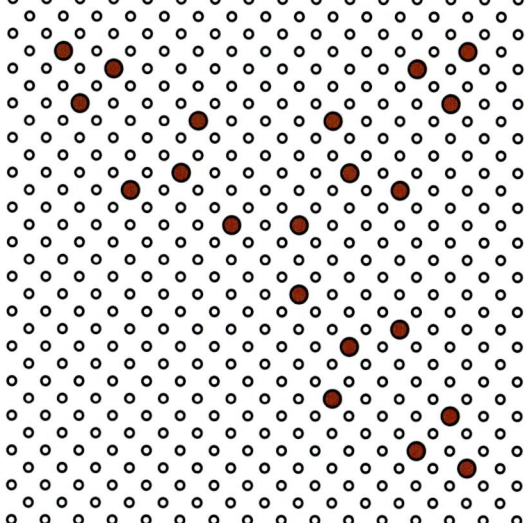

SMALL FLOWER WRAP

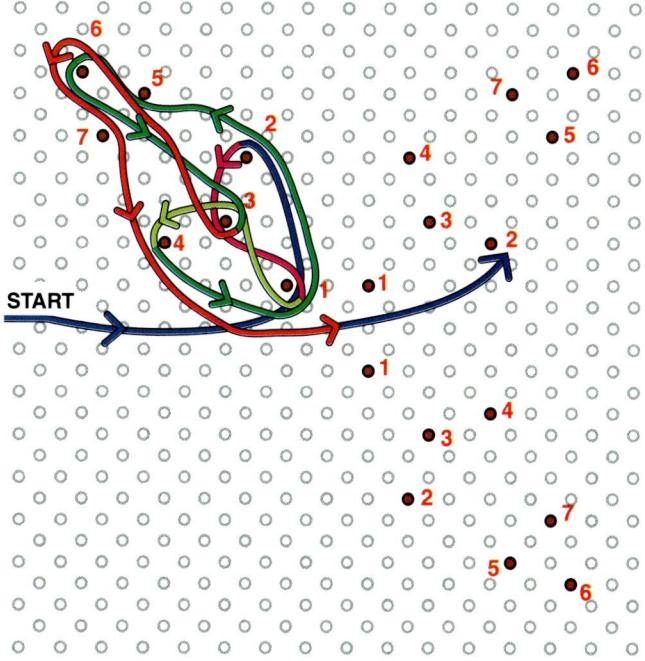

Christmas Dinner Recipes

Photo on pages 58 and 59

by Kenna Prior

ORANGE GLAZED CORNISH HENS

4 cornish hens
3 oz. of frozen orange juice concentrate
4 sprigs of fresh tarragon
4 fresh mint leaves
¼ cup fresh mint, chopped
¼ cup fresh rosemary, chopped
Small can of mandarin orange slices, drained
1 teaspoon salt
1 teaspoon ground black pepper

Preheat oven to 350°.

To prepare each hen, tie the legs together with cotton twine. Using your finger, lift the skin on the breast, being careful not to tear. Insert a sprig of tarragon and a mint leaf under the skin.

Combine ¼ cup each chopped rosemary and mint; mix together (½ cup). Divide the mixture into fourths and place one fourth inside the cavity of each hen.

Place the hens in a baking dish and bake uncovered for 1 hour.

Glaze: While the hens are baking, combine the frozen orange juice, salt and pepper in a mixing bowl.

After the hens have baked for 1 hour, baste the hens with the glaze mixture.

Bake for an additional 15 minutes and baste again; repeat until hens are done.

To Serve: Remove from oven and place on a warm serving plate (reserve broth to use in the dressing).

Garnish with mint leaves, mandarin orange slices and grape tomatoes.

CRANBERRY DRESSING

1 cup whole berry cranberry sauce
10 slices of whole wheat bread
1 hard-boiled egg, chopped
2 eggs, beaten
1 teaspoon salt
¼ cup freshly chopped tarragon
½ cup freshly chopped mint
3 oz. of frozen orange juice concentrate
¾ cup chopped green onions
½ to 1 cup broth reserved from cornish hens or chicken broth

Preheat oven to 350°.

Cube 10 slices of wheat bread and bake at 350° for 10 to 15 minutes. Remove from oven and let cool.

In a large bowl, combine the bread cubes, the undiluted orange juice, the chopped hard-boiled egg, the green onions, tarragon, mint, and salt.

Carefully and evenly stir in the broth. Let stand 10 minutes, then stir again.

Add the cranberry sauce and the beaten eggs and stir again.

Place in a greased 2 quart casserole dish and bake for 45 to 60 minutes, or until firm in the center.

CHRISTMAS SALAD

Mix salad greens (baby lettuce, endive & mustard greens)
¾ cup pine nuts
Package of ramen noodles (dry — discard seasoning packet)
1 cup grape tomatoes
¾ cup rice vinegar

Pour salad greens into a large bowl; tear leaves into smaller pieces as desired.

Right before serving, crumble the noodles over the salad greens and toss.

Pour rice vinegar over all and toss again.

Sprinkle pine nuts and tomatoes over top and serve.

SAGE SKILLET CORN

4 fresh ears of corn
½ cup heavy cream or half and half
½ stick butter
¼ cup fresh sage, chopped
½ teaspoon salt

Partially shuck corn, removing the silk and leaving the husks pulled up.

Using the husks as a handle, stand each ear of corn on a cutting board and use a large knife to slice downward against the cob to remove the kernels; then scrape the cob with the knife to remove the remainder of the kernels.

Combine the corn, butter and cream in a heavy skillet, cook at medium high for about 15 minutes or until hot and cream has cooked down.

Add the chopped sage and the salt, stir well and remove from heat.

SUGAR SNAP PEAS WITH PEARL ONIONS

1 lb. fresh sugar snap peas
10 to 12 pearl onions
½ cup chicken broth
Salt to taste

Wash peas and remove any stems and tips which are brown or tough.

Trim off the root and stem ends of the onions, peel and wash.

Place the chicken broth, peas and onions in a saucepan, bring to a simmer and cook until peas are tender-crisp, but before soft or limp. Add salt to taste.

PUMPKIN NUT BREAD

1 cup sugar
¼ teaspoon baking powder
½ teaspoon salt
½ teaspoon each allspice, cinnamon, nutmeg
1¾ cup flour
½ cup oil
½ cup water
½ cup canned pumpkin
½ cup chopped pecans
Whipped topping (see recipe on page 63)

Preheat oven to 400°
Combine sugar, spices and pumpkin together in large

bowl. Add oil and water and mix thoroughly. Slowly add flour ½ cup at a time and mix, then add nuts.

Oil and flour one loaf pan. Pour the mixture into the loaf pan and bake at 400° for 45 minutes to 1 hour.

Remove from oven and leave in pan. Tilt pan to one side and allow to cool 20 minutes, then tilt to the other side for 20 minutes. Flip loaf out of the pan onto a wire rack to finish cooling.

To serve: Slice; top with whipped topping (Wilton decorating bag with tip #21 shown), sprinkle with pecans.

WHIPPED TOPPING

3 oz. package cream cheese, softened
1½ cups powdered sugar
½ stick butter, softened
¼ tsp. vanilla
2 tablespoons heavy cream
1 tablespoon frozen orange juice concentrate, thawed

Cream together butter, cream cheese and vanilla.

Blend in the cream and the orange juice concentrate; whip until light and fluffy. Gradually add powdered sugar a little at a time and blend thoroughly.

Bow and Holly Mosaic Tray
Continued from page 49

cutting tiles; take extra care when handling the broken tiles as the edges will be very sharp.

3: To break the tiles into ¼" to ½" pieces, lay a thick towel on a solid work surface. On one half of the towel, spread out the tiles to be broken with the colored side of the tiles facing down; fold the remaining half of the towel over the tiles. Using the hammer, hit the tiles with just enough force to break them into desired sizes. Lift the towel after every few hits to check your progress. For more precise cuts, the tiles can be trimmed to fit using the tile nipper.

4: To glue the tile chips in place on the bottom of the tray, use the craft stick to spread out a thin layer of adhesive over one section at a time. Leaving about ⅛" between tile pieces to make room for the grout, spread the adhesive inside the bow and streamer outlines and glue down the red tile chips.

5: Spread the glue inside the holly leaf outlines and glue down the green tile chips.

6: For the berries, spread a small amount of glue on the backs of four red tile chips and randomly glue them in place around the holly leaves *(see photo)*.

7: Using both methods of gluing as needed, glue white tile chips in the remaining area surrounding the bow and holly leaves. Let the glue dry overnight.

8: Mix the grout according to the manufacturer's instructions. Using the spatula, spread the grout over the top of the tiles, pressing it into the spaces between the tiles. Fill in all the spaces, bringing the level of the grout up even with the top of the tiles.

9: Gently wipe the grout off the top of the tiles with a slightly damp sponge or rag, being careful not to remove any grout from between the tiles and expose the sharp edges. Let the grout dry overnight.

10: With a dry cloth, wipe off any grout residue on the tiles and the wooden tray. Paint the sides of the tray with green paint; let dry. Apply additional coats as needed for complete coverage.

11: Paint a thin layer of varnish over the green painted area only; let dry. Apply as many additional coats of varnish as desired.

Luminarias

Designed by Blanche Lind

For use with votive candleholder and candles

Poinsettia

Finished Size:
   4" wide x 8½" tall.

Materials:
   ❏ 2 sheets of 8½" x 11" crafting plastic
   ❏ 4 paper napkins with poinsettia design
   ❏ 2 sheets of white tissue paper
   ❏ Tulip® Dimensional Craft Paint by Duncan Enterprises:
      Slick® True Red #65130
      Slick® Leaf Green #65032
      Pearl® Soft Yellow #65045
   ❏ Gold glitter slivers
   ❏ 2 yds. of gold metallic ¼"-wide rickrack
   ❏ Scissors
   ❏ Stapler
   ❏ Foam brush
   ❏ Reversible Collage Glue by Aleene's™
   ❏ Thick Designer Tacky Glue by Aleene's™

Note:
   Never leave a burning candle unattended. Always place candles in a heat-safe container such as a glass votive.

Instructions

1: Trim each of the plastic sheets to measure 8½" square.

2: On each sheet, fold one side over ½" and crease it by rubbing the handle of the scissors over it two or three times *(see First Fold illustration)*. In the same manner, fold the opposite edge of the sheet even with the first fold and crease the sheet with the scissors *(see Second Fold illustration)*.

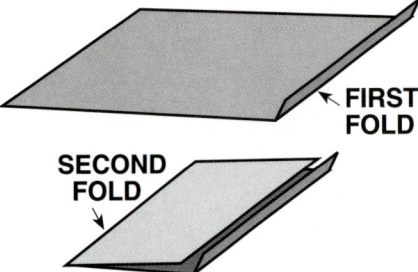

3: Make sure the two sheets fit together properly by standing both sheets upright with the ½" fold on one sheet overlapping the unfolded edge of the other sheet. They should form a rectangular tube 8½" tall and 4" square *(see Tube illustration)*.

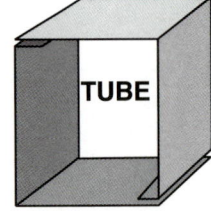

Continued on page 76

Beaded Evening Bag

Designed by Carole Rodgers

Finished Size:
Bag is 7" x 8", plus Drawstring and Beaded Fringe.

Materials:
- Clear silver-lined glass beads:
    2 hanks *(about 7,600 beads)* of size 11° seed
    108 of 4 mm x 4 mm square
- Black opaque glass beads:
    796 of size 8° seed
    18 E beads
    54 of 8 mm-diameter disk
- Black faceted glass beads:
    38 of 4 mm round
    18 of 6 mm round
    18 of 8 mm x 10 mm oval
    18 of 9 mm x 7 mm teardrop
- Fabric:
    2 pieces each 7½" x 10¼" of black satin
    2 pieces each 7½" x 8" of black lining
- 48" of black 5 mm twisted satin cord
- Sewing needle and black thread
- Sewing machine *(optional)*
- Bead sorting tray
- Size 10 beading needle
- White beading thread
- Scissors
- Straight pins
- Bodkin or large safety pin

Beaded Cover

1: Thread the beading needle with about 1½ yds. of beading thread. Do not double the thread; use a single strand throughout.

2: Pour clear silver-lined seed beads and black opaque seed beads into separate compartments in the bead sorting tray.

3: For the **first strand,** thread on one black bead, slide to about 5" from the end and tie a loose knot around the bead that can be untied later.

4: Thread on five silver beads and one black bead; repeat this sequence until you have 95 silver beads and 20 black beads *(see illustration No. 1)*, then thread on one more silver bead *(this is a point bead)* and run the needle back through the last black bead in the opposite direction.

5: For the **next strand,** thread on five silver beads, one black bead and five silver beads; skip one black bead on the previous strand and run the needle through the next black bead *(see illustrations No. 2 and No. 3)*; repeat this sequence until you have 90 silver beads and 19 black beads, then thread on five silver beads, one black bead and one silver bead *(this is a point bead)*; run the needle back through the last black bead in the opposite direction.

6: Repeat step 5 until you have a total of 75 strands.

7: For the **joining strand,** work as follows:
   A: Thread on five silver beads, skip the black bead next to the point bead on the first strand and run the needle through the next black bead on the first strand

Continued on page 78

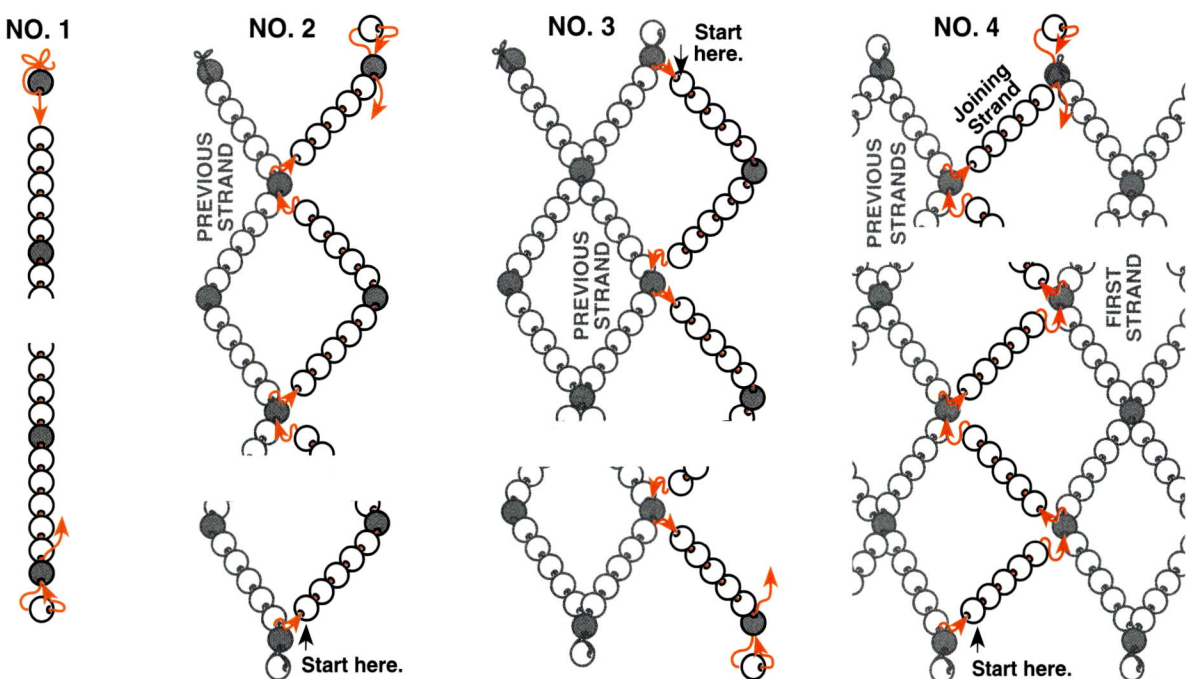

Entertaining Delights ~ page 67

Five Golden Rings Table Wreath

Designed by Sylvia Montroy

Finished Size:
Wreath is 15" high; greenery covers about 12" x 30".

Materials:
- 2 heart-shaped 12" foam wreaths
- 1" x 4" x 10" Styrofoam® block
- 24"-long artificial Canadian pine centerpiece swag
- 24 artificial pine sprigs each 4" long
- Silk English ivy vines:
    - 30 vines each 6" long
    - 12 vines each 9" long
    - 12 vines each 14" long
- 12 red 4"-long berry clusters
- 2 gold 4"-tall cherub ornaments
- 5 gold 1"-diameter rings *(metal or plastic)*
- 10" of gold $5/8$"-wide metallic ribbon
- 8 yds. of gold $1\frac{1}{2}$"-wide metallic ribbon
- 2 yds. of red/gold 3"-wide wire-edge ribbon
- $1/8$" wooden dowel:
    - 4 pieces each 2" long
    - 4 pieces each 4" long
- 2 red 12"-long chenille stems
- 54 floral pins
- Wire cutters
- Ruler
- Serrated knife
- Scissors
- Low temperature glue gun and glue sticks

Instructions

1: To join the two foam hearts, lay one heart flat on a solid work surface and place the second heart directly on top of the first heart with edges matching. Evenly spacing two dowels on each side of the top heart, push the 2" dowels through the top heart and down into the bottom heart *(see illustration on page 79)*. Apply a bead of glue around the outer seam where the hearts meet for added stability.

2: With the serrated knife, cut off about 2" horizontally from the point of the attached hearts *(see illustration)*.

3: Apply glue around one end of each 4"-long dowel, insert one dowel about 1" deep into each cut end of each heart *(see illustration)*.

4: Beginning at one cut end of the heart and ending at the other cut end, tightly wrap the $1\frac{1}{2}$" gold ribbon around the assembled heart, overlapping the edges slightly to hide the foam. Trim off any excess ribbon; secure both ends of the ribbon to the heart with glue.

5: Glue six or seven of the 4" pine sprigs around the 1" outer sides of the foam block *(base)* covering the foam.

6: Center the swag over the *base*, apply a generous amount

Continued on page 79

Entertaining Delights ~ page 69

Christmas Desserts

Recipes on pages 75 and 76

Entertaining Delights - page 70

Old-World Finial Topiary and Candleholders

Designed by Sylvia Montroy
Instructions on pages 72-75

Old-World Finial Topiary and Candleholders

Photo on pages 70 and 71

Topiary

Finished Size:
About 21¼" tall.

Materials for Topiary:
- 5" x 12" Styrofoam® cone
- 100 yds. crochet cotton thread *(any color)*
- Renaissance Foil™ Products by Delta Technical Coatings:
    - Silver Foil packet *(to cover 720 square inches)*
    - 2 oz. Pewter Gray Base Coat
    - 2 oz. Adhesive
    - 2 oz. Silver Tarnish Antique *(antiquing solution)*
- Ceramcoat® Products by Delta Technical Coatings:
    - 3 oz. Artist Gesso
    - Satin Finish Interior Spray Varnish
    - Gloss Finish Exterior Varnish *(fast drying)*
- 3¾"-diameter wooden coaster
- 2 wooden 2⅛" x 1¾" egg cups
- Graber® 4¼" Natural Wooden Finial #3-541-0 by Spring Window Fashions Division, Inc.
- 3½" x 3½" x ¾" wooden block
- 12" long wooden dowel *(same size as metal stud in wooden finial)*
- 2½ yds. ¼"-wide single-loop braided trim *(any color)*
- ½ yd. ¼"-wide double-loop braided trim *(any color)*
- 30 assorted silver and silver/white buttons
- 12 white 10 mm pearl beads
- 3" x 60" piece of gray fiberglass screening
- 36" of black 30-gauge cloth-covered wire
- Disposable paint palette or foam plate
- Paintbrushes:
    - ½" varnish
    - ½" flat
- Electric drill with drill bit *(same size as metal stud in wooden finial)*
- Sandpaper
- Tack cloth
- Hand saw
- Scissors
- Old toothbrush
- Ruler
- Dressmaker pins *(large head)*
- Paper towels
- Serrated knife
- Toothpicks
- Wire cutters
- Pliers
- Soft cloth
- Crafty Magic Melt® Craft & Floral Pro™ Glue Gun by Adhesive Technologies
- Crafty Magic Melt® Jewelry Glue by Adhesive Technologies
- Quik 'n Tacky™ Craft Glue by Delta Technical Coatings

Note:
Read all instructions thoroughly before beginning.

Instructions

1: With the pliers, remove the metal stud attached to the finial and discard it. With the serrated knife, cut ¾" from the top of the foam cone to create a flat surface for the finial to sit on. If necessary, the removed cone tip can be used to rub smooth any rough edges.

2: With the drill bit, drill out the existing hole in the finial to a depth of about 1".

3: Using the same drill bit, drill a hole through the center of the wooden coaster and through the center of both wooden egg cups. Drill a hole ½" deep into the center of the 3½" square wooden block — **do not drill completely through the bottom of the block.**

4: With the hand saw, cut the dowel into one 3" piece and one 9" piece.

5: Sand the edges and holes on each wooden piece and wipe them clean with the tack cloth.

6: Insert the 3" dowel vertically about 2" deep into the center of the cone top. Insert the 9" dowel vertically about 2" deep into the center of the cone bottom.

7: Leaving both dowels in place to keep the holes in the foam clear and to hold thread in place, begin wrapping the crochet thread vertically around the cone. Wrap the thread tight enough that it cuts into the top and bottom edges of the foam about 1/16". For added interest and texture, occasionally cross the threads. Secure both ends of the thread with glue. Remove the 9" dowel from the cone.

8: To assemble the wooden base, hot glue one end of the 9" dowel into the 3½" square block. Apply a generous line of craft glue around the inside rim of one egg cup; turn the cup upside down and slip it over the dowel and onto the block. Apply a line of craft glue to the bottoms of both egg cups. Slip the remaining egg cup right-side-up over the dowel and line up the bottom edges of the two cups. Allow to dry for several minutes.

9: Apply a generous line of craft glue around the inside rim of the second egg cup; slip the coaster over the dowel and onto the egg cup, turn the entire base upside down so that the glue runs down onto the coaster. Prop the base upside down on the work surface and allow to dry for several minutes.

10: Being careful not to disturb the threads, remove the 3" dowel from the top of the cone. Apply craft glue to the hole in the finial and to the top 1" of the dowel; insert the glued end of the dowel into the finial.

11: Apply a generous amount of hot glue to the top of the cone, covering the threads. Insert the opposite end of the 3" dowel into the top of the cone making sure the finial is sitting straight and level on the cone.

12: In the same manner, glue the coaster on top of the wooden base to the bottom of the cone.

13: Cutting each piece of trim to fit as needed, glue single-loop braided trim in place on the finial with craft glue as follows *(see photo)*:
  A: Around the top of the large center ball.
  B: Around the bottom of the large center ball.
  C: Around the base of the finial over the top of the cone.

14: Cutting each piece of trim to fit as needed, glue single-

Entertaining Delights ~ page 72

loop braided trim in place on the assembled base with craft glue as follows *(see photo)*:

A: Around the top egg cup where it is glued to the coaster.

B: Around the two egg cups where they are glued together.

C: Around the top outer edge of the wooden block.

D: Around the top edge on the side of the wooden block.

E: Around the bottom edge on the side of the wooden block.

15: Cut a piece of double-loop braided trim to fit around the bottom edge of the cone *(see photo)*; glue in place with craft glue. If necessary, use dressmaker pins to secure the trim while the glue dries. Set the Topiary aside until all glue is dry, then remove pins.

16: Using the varnish brush, apply a generous coat of gesso to the finial, the cone and the wooden base, covering the threads and using a gentle dabbing motion to get it into the crevices of the cone and trim. Let dry overnight.

17: In the same manner, with the varnish brush, cover all surfaces with the gray base coat. Let dry.

18: With the flat brush, following the manufacturer's instructions, apply a coat of adhesive to all surfaces; let the adhesive dry until clear. Apply a second coat and let dry until clear.

19: Working on a clean, dry work surface, cut the foil into 6" squares for easier handling. Gently lift one piece of foil and lay it against one area on the cone. With your fingers, lightly press the foil against the adhesive; use a toothpick to press the foil into the crevices of the cone and between the threads. Repeat this process until most of the Topiary has been covered while allowing some of the base coat to show through. If the foil does not adhere in some areas, apply another coat of adhesive to that area, let it dry until clear and reapply the foil.

20: Use the old toothbrush to gently brush away any small pieces of loose foil.

21: Working in one small area at a time with the varnish brush, apply a light coat of exterior varnish to all foiled surfaces. If the varnish is too thick or bubbles up, remove the excess with the tip of the brush and wipe it off on a paper towel. Let dry.

22: With the varnish brush, apply the antiquing solution to one small area of the cone, working it into the crevices with a dabbing motion as before. Use the soft cloth to gently wipe some of the antiquing from the top of the threads, leaving it darker in the crevices. Repeat this process around the entire cone and on the braided trim.

23: Dip a corner of the soft cloth into the antiquing solution and dab it over the finial, blotting away any excess with a clean piece of the cloth. In the same manner, apply the antiquing solution to the base of the Topiary. Dry thoroughly.

24: Working in a well ventilated area, apply a light coat of the interior spray varnish to seal the finish. Let dry.

25: Apply another coat of exterior varnish to the entire Topiary as in step 21.

26: To make the screen garland, lay the screen flat on the work surface, gather one short end and tightly wrap the gathered end with a 2½" piece of cloth-covered wire. Twist the ends of the wire and trim off the excess with wire cutters. Continue gathering the screen in this manner about every four inches, allowing the screen to pouf out between the gathers.

27: Place the first gathered end of the screen just below the finial and pin to the cone with one or two dressmaker pins. Securing each of the gathers with dressmaker pins, drape the garland in a spiral around the cone ending at the base of the cone. Adjust the garland as desired; trim off any excess garland. Place a drop of hot glue at each of the gathers for additional stability.

28: Hot glue three or four buttons and pearls over the wire at each gathered area as desired.

Candleholders

Finished Sizes:
Candleholders range 7¼" tall to 11¼" tall.

Basic Materials for Each Candleholder:
❑ Renaissance Foil™ Products by Delta Technical Coatings:
   7 ft.-long piece of Silver Foil
   2 oz. Adhesive
   2 oz. Pewter Gray Base Coat
   2 oz. Silver Tarnish Antique *(antiquing solution)*
❑ Ceramcoat® Products by Delta Technical Coatings:
   2 oz. Artist Gesso
   2 oz. Gloss Finish Exterior Varnish
   Satin Finish Interior Spray Varnish
❑ Paintbrushes:
   ½" varnish
   ½" flat
❑ Scissors
❑ Pencil
❑ Ruler
❑ Toothpicks
❑ Tack cloth
❑ Sandpaper
❑ Paper towels
❑ Soft cloth
❑ Old toothbrush
❑ Wire cutters
❑ Crafty Magic Melt® Craft & Floral Pro™ Glue Gun by Adhesive Technologies
❑ Crafty Magic Melt® Jewelry Glue by Adhesive Technologies
❑ Quik 'n Tacky™ Craft Glue by Delta Technical Coatings

Additional Materials for Small Candleholder:
❑ 2¼" x 5½" wooden milk bottle
❑ 2½" x ¾" wooden wheel
❑ 3½" x 3½" x ¾" wooden block
❑ 3½"-diameter wooden or plastic beverage coaster
❑ 30" strand of 4 mm pearls *(any color)*
❑ 32 plastic holly leaves *(about 1" long)*
❑ 36 plastic 6 mm faceted beads *(any color)*

Additional Materials for Medium Candleholder:
❑ 6¾" tall wooden candlestick
❑ 2½" x ¾" wooden wheel
❑ 3½" x 3½" x ¾" wooden block

Continued on page 74

Old-World Finial Topiary and Candleholders

Continued from page 73

- ❑ 3½"-diameter wooden or plastic beverage coaster
- ❑ 30" strand of 4 mm pearls *(any color)*
- ❑ 26 plastic holly leaves *(about 1" long)*
- ❑ 30 plastic 6 mm faceted beads *(any color)*

Additional Materials for Large Candleholder:
- ❑ 9" tall wooden candlestick
- ❑ 2½" x ¾" wooden wheel
- ❑ 3½" x 3½" x ¾" wooden block
- ❑ 3½"-diameter wooden or plastic beverage coaster
- ❑ 30" strand of 4 mm pearls *(any color)*
- ❑ 26 plastic holly leaves *(about 1" long)*
- ❑ 30 plastic 6 mm faceted beads *(any color)*

Basic Foiling & Finishing (use with instructions for individual Candleholders)

1: After the Candleholders have been completely assembled, remove any hot glue threads and wipe Candleholders clean.
2: Using the varnish brush, apply a generous coat of gesso to all surfaces. Use a dabbing motion to get in behind the leaves and between the beads. Let dry overnight.
3: In the same manner, with the varnish brush, cover all surfaces with the gray base coat. Let dry.
4: With the flat artist's brush, following the manufacturer's instructions, apply a coat of adhesive to all surfaces. Let the adhesive dry until clear and apply a second coat. Let the second coat dry until clear.
5: Working on a clean, dry work surface, cut the foil into 6" squares for easier handling. Gently lift one piece of the foil and lay it against one area at a time. With your fingers, lightly press the foil against the adhesive; use a toothpick to press the foil into the crevices around leaves, berries and beads. Repeat this process until most of the Candleholder has been covered while allowing some of the base coat to show through. If the foil does not adhere in some areas, apply another coat of adhesive to that area, let it dry until clear and reapply the foil.
6: Use an old toothbrush to gently brush away any small pieces of loose foil.
7: Working in one small area at a time, apply a light coat of exterior varnish to all foiled surfaces with the varnish brush. If the varnish is too thick or bubbles up, remove the excess with the tip of the brush and wipe it off on a paper towel. Let dry.
8: With the varnish brush, apply the antiquing solution to one small area of the Candleholder, working it into the crevices with a dabbing motion as before. Use the soft cloth to gently wipe some of the antiquing from the surface of the leaves, berries and beads, leaving it darker in the crevices. Repeat this process around the entire Candleholder. Dry thoroughly.
9: Working in a well ventilated area, apply a light coat of the spray varnish to seal the finish. Let dry.
10: Apply another coat of exterior varnish to the entire Candleholder as in step 7.

Small Candleholder

1: With sandpaper, smooth any rough edges on the wood pieces and remove the sanding dust with the tack cloth.
2: Using hot glue to assemble the wooden pieces, glue the bottom of the milk bottle to the center of the block; glue the wheel centered on the top of the milk bottle; glue the coaster centered on top of the wheel *(see photo)*.
3: To apply the pearls, cut a length of pearls to fit around each glue joint between the coaster and wheel, between the wheel and milk bottle, and between the milk bottle and block *(see photo)*. Cut another length of pearls to fit around the neck of the milk bottle. Apply a thin bead of craft glue around each joint and lay the pearls in place. Let dry.
4: With wire cutters, cut the holly leaves from the main branch and trim off the stems. Make eight clusters each with two leaves and three beads *(see Two Leaf Cluster illustration)*; hot glue two clusters to each side of the wooden block *(see photo)*.

5: Make four clusters each with three leaves and three beads *(see Three Leaf Cluster illustration)*; hot glue these evenly spaced around the milk bottle about 1" below the neck of the bottle *(see photo)*.
6: Hot glue a single leaf on top of each corner of the wooden block with the stem next to the pearls and the tip of the leaf pointing toward the corner of the block *(see photo)*.
7: Work steps 1–10 of the Basic Foiling and Finishing.

Medium & Large Candleholders

1: With sandpaper, smooth any rough edges on the wooden pieces and remove the sanding dust with the tack cloth.
2: Using hot glue to assemble the wooden pieces, glue the bottom of the candlestick to the center of the block, glue the wheel to the top of the candlestick and glue the coaster centered on top of the wheel *(see photo)*.
3: To apply the pearls, cut lengths of pearls as needed to fit around the glue joints between the coaster and wheel, between the wheel and candlestick, and between the candlestick and block. Apply a thin bead of craft glue around each joint and lay the pearls in place. Apply any remaining pearls as desired. Let dry.
4: With wire cutters, cut the holly leaves from the main branch and trim off the stems. Make eight clusters each with two leaves and three beads *(see Two Leaf Cluster illustration)*; hot glue two clusters to each side of the block *(see photo)*.
5: Hot glue a single leaf on top of each corner of the block with the stem next to the pearls and the tip of the leaf pointing toward the corner of the block *(see photo)*.
6: Make two clusters each with three leaves and three beads *(see Three Leaf Cluster illustration)*; hot glue these to each side of the Candleholder as desired *(see photo)*.
7: Work steps 1–10 of the Basic Foiling and Finishing instructions.

Christmas Dessert Recipes

Photo on pages 70 and 71

by Linda Moll Smith

ORANGE TANGELO AND CRANBERRY SALAD
A refreshing and spirited counterpoint to sweeter desserts.

6 Mineola (large) tangelos, washed well and dried
¼ cup sugar
1 tablespoon cinnamon
1 tablespoon dried orange peel, diced
1¼ cup fresh or frozen whole cranberries, rinsed and picked over
1¾ cup sugar, divided
1 large can mandarin orange segments
1 cup of any orange-flavored liqueur
2 tablespoons fresh lemon juice
Sprigs of fresh rosemary (for garnish)

Prepare the tangelo shells: Slice tangelos in half.
Using a sharp knife, slice around and between segments to loosen. Empty into bowl, discarding all membranes. Completely clean out shells, scraping with a spoon if necessary.
Drain segments and pour juice into shallow bowl.
In another dish, combine the ¼ cup sugar, cinnamon and dried orange peel.
Dip cut edge of each shell into the juice and then into the sugar mixture, coating the edge of each shell. Refrigerate shells.

Make the salad: Combine cranberries, 1½ cups of sugar and ¾ cup of orange liqueur in a small, heavy saucepan. Bring to a boil, stirring occasionally; boil for one minute and remove from heat. Allow to cool.
Mix drained mandarin orange segments with tangelo segments.
Combine remaining ¼ cup sugar, remaining ¼ cup orange liqueur and 2 tablespoons lemon juice; pour over the orange and tangelo segments, toss gently and allow to marinate for a few minutes.

To serve: Drain the juice from the orange and tangelo segments and spoon equal portions into the 12 orange shells.
Generously garnish each serving with the cooked cranberries.
Arrange on a tray garnished with sprigs of rosemary.
Best served chilled. Makes one dozen.

SUGAR PLUMS
After the buffet is over, visions of these will be dancing in your guests' heads.

24–30 red (or green) whole maraschino cherries with stems, drained well
½ cup dried apricots, finely chopped
¼ cup dried pitted prunes, finely chopped
¼ cup golden raisins
½ cup walnuts, finely chopped
¼ cup sweetened, grated coconut
2–3 tablespoons apricot brandy
¼ cup red crystallized sugar

Finely chop all ingredients by hand, or in a food processor.
Blend fruits, nuts and coconut together with about 2 tablespoons brandy — just enough to moisten, adding a third tablespoonful only if necessary to hold ingredients together.
Pressing firmly, form a ball of the chopped mixture around each cherry, leaving the stem sticking out.
Roll the ball gently in sugar crystals to coat.
Store in the refrigerator for up to a month in an airtight container, placing the balls in layers with wax paper between.
To serve: Mound into a pyramid on a doily-lined tray.
Makes about 2 dozen 1½" balls.

BIT O' SHERRY TRIFLE
A shortcut version of this essentially English layered dessert uses ready-made ingredients to bypass hours of preparation.

Loaf of pound cake
3 tablespoons fruit preserves or jam, any flavor (black currant or raspberry is traditional)
16-ounce can sliced fruit (any kind), drained and juice reserved, or fresh fruit, such as raspberries or strawberries
¼ cup sweet sherry
2 cups vanilla pudding
1 pint whipped cream (or whipped topping)
Choice of nuts, candied cherries and crystallized ginger or angelica (for garnish)

Cut cake into 8 to 10 slices; spread preserves between two slices to make 4 or 5 sandwiches. Cut each sandwich into quarters.
Arrange cubes of cake sandwiches in a layer on the bottom of a glass trifle bowl or flat-bottomed glass salad bowl.
Mix juice from the fruit with sherry and pour over the cake pieces.
Layer fruit over the cake and spread vanilla pudding over top of the fruit.
Spread whipped cream or topping evenly over the pudding and garnish as desired with nuts, candied cherries and crystallized ginger or angelica.
Refrigerate until ready to use. Serve in glass bowls like a pudding the same day it is made.
Serves 10–12.

EGGNOG
This is a a holiday essential.

2 quarts milk
1½ cups sugar
¼ cup all-purpose flour
⅛ teaspoon salt
4 large eggs, plus 2 egg whites
2 teaspoons vanilla

Continued on page 76

Beverage Tips

- Mix defrosted lemonade with two cans of cold water. Freeze in ice trays and use in punch drinks or apple cider.
- Freeze berries or mint sprigs into ice cubes: Freeze ½ of the liquid, add berry, and freeze again. Add remaining liquid and freeze until solid. Look for ice molds in Christmas shapes.
- Insert a fresh flower stem into a citrus round and float in a punch.
- Cloved lemons and oranges add color and flavor to a hot or cold cider bowl.
- Float an ice mold, flavored ice, colored ice cubes … in punch.
- Allow one pound of ice per person when serving cocktails.

Christmas Dessert Recipes
Continued from page 75

½ cup rum (optional)
Nutmeg and whipped cream, if desired, for garnish

Heat the milk over low to medium heat until scalded. Set aside.

In another saucepan, stir together sugar, flour and salt. Add eggs and egg whites and whisk until blended well.

Gradually stir in scalded milk.

Cook over low heat, stirring constantly, until the custard has thickened enough to coat a spoon (about 15 minutes). Remove from heat and stir in vanilla.

Cover and chill, preferably overnight. Makes two quarts.

To serve: Stir in rum, if using, and whip the mixture gently until frothy, adding a little ice water if it is too thick.

Pour into mugs or glasses, top with whipped cream and sprinkle on nutmeg.

Luminarias
Continued from page 64

4: Cut two 9" x 12" pieces of tissue paper; gently crumple each sheet of paper into a ball then smooth it out slightly.

5: Using the foam brush, apply an even layer of collage glue on the inside of both plastic sheets. Sprinkle gold glitter slivers over the entire area.

6: While the glue is still wet, cover the inside of each plastic sheet with one piece of tissue paper. Apply another coat of collage glue over the paper. Let dry.

7: Trim the tissue paper even with the edges of the plastic sheets.

8: Cut four large, four medium and four small poinsettias from the paper napkins. Remove the back layer of napkin from each flower.

9: Working on the front side of the folded plastic sheets, starting at the top, glue one small, one medium and one large flower on each section using collage glue *(see photo)*.

10: Carefully apply a coat of collage glue over all of the flowers. Let dry.

11: With the red paint, outline the petals of each flower. Place several small dots of yellow and green paint at the center of each flower.

12: With green paint, outline each leaf and randomly paint pine sprays as desired *(see photo)*.

13: For the berries, randomly place dots of red paint around the pine sprays.

14: To assemble the luminaria, stand both sheets of plastic upright with the smaller flowers at the top. Apply tacky glue to the outside of both ½" folds; on each side, place the unfolded edge of one sheet on top of the ½" fold of the other sheet *(see Tube illustration — the folded edge goes on the inside of the luminaria)*. Staple the top and bottom of each seam.

15: Cut a piece of rickrack to fit around the top and bottom of the luminaria; glue each piece in place with the tacky glue *(see photo)*.

Christmas Tree

Finished Size:
3½" across and 6¼" tall.

Materials:
- Sheet of 8½" x 11" crafting plastic
- 3 paper napkins with Christmas tree design
- Sheet of dark blue tissue paper
- Tulip® Dimensional Craft Paint by Duncan Enterprises:
    Glitter Ruby #65114
    Glitter Silver #65089
    Glitter Gold #65088
    Slick® Leaf Green #65032
- Dimensional Snow Textured Medium by Duncan Enterprises
- 3 gold sequin stars
- Iridescent glitter
- Decorative scissors
- Craft stick
- Scissors
- Stapler
- Foam brush
- Reversible Collage Glue by Aleene's™
- Thick Designer Tacky Glue by Aleene's™

Note:
Never leave a burning candle unattended. Always place candles in a heat-safe container such as a glass votive.

Instructions

1: Trim the plastic sheet to measure 7" x 11".
2: Crumple the sheet of tissue paper into a ball then smooth it out to fit over the plastic sheet.
3: Using the foam brush, apply an even layer of collage glue on one side of the plastic sheet. Sprinkle iridescent glitter over the entire area.
4: While the glue is still wet, cover the inside of the sheet with the tissue paper. Apply another coat of collage glue over the paper. Let dry.
5: Trim the tissue paper even with the edges of the plastic sheet.
6: Cut out three Christmas trees from the paper napkins; remove the back layer of napkin from each.
7: With the bottom of the trees about 1" from the bottom edge of the plastic, glue the trees evenly spaced across the other side of the plastic using the collage glue.
8: Carefully apply a coat of collage glue over the trees. Let dry.
9: With the red and gold glitter paints, decorate the ornaments on the trees as desired. Decorate the garlands on the trees with the silver glitter paint.
10: Use the tacky glue to glue one gold star to the top of each tree.
11: With the craft stick, spread a generous layer of snow medium across the bottom of the plastic around and under the trees *(see photo)*. Let dry.
12: With the decorative scissors, remove about ¾" around the top edge of the plastic sheet.
13: Roll the plastic sheet into a cylinder, overlapping the ends about ½"; secure the seam with tacky glue and staple the top and bottom of the seam.

Madonna

Finished Size:
3½" across and 8½" tall.

Materials:
- Sheet of 8½" x 11" crafting plastic
- Sheet of gold foil by Aleene's™
- Sheet each of yellow, royal blue, light blue, pink, mauve, dark green and cream tissue paper
- 12" of flat ¾"-wide decorative trim
- Cotton swabs
- Pencil
- Toothpicks
- Transparent tape
- Scissors
- Stapler
- Foam brush
- Tracing paper and pencil
- 3-D Foiling Glue by Aleene's™
- Reversible Collage Glue by Aleene's™
- Thick Designer Tacky Glue by Aleene's™

Note:
Never leave a burning candle unattended. Always place candles in a heat-safe container such as a glass votive.

Instructions

1: Trace the Madonna *(blue lines)* onto tracing paper. Lay the plastic sheet centered over the Madonna pattern and tape it in place.
2: Using the photo as a color guide, make individual pattern pieces from the colored tissue paper as follows: For the **halos,** lay a sheet of yellow tissue paper on top of the plastic over the pattern; trace over the outlines of the Madonna and child halos. Cut out the pieces. In the same manner, make the remaining pieces of the Madonna pattern.
3: With the foam brush, carefully spread collage glue on the back of each pattern piece; lay each piece in place on top of the plastic sheet to form the design.
4: Apply another coat of collage glue to the entire pattern. Use the cotton swabs to wipe away any glue from the plastic around the pattern. Let dry.
5: With the 3-D foiling glue, outline all of the pattern pieces *(see photo)*. If necessary, straighten up the outlines with a toothpick. Let dry overnight.
6: Place the gold foil sheet over the glued outlines, shiny side up, and rub gently with your finger or a craft stick to transfer the gold foil.
7: Remove the Madonna pattern from the back of the plastic sheet.
8: Crumple the white tissue paper then smooth the paper out to fit the plastic sheet.
9: Working on the back side of the plastic sheet, apply a coat of collage glue to the entire surface of the sheet with the foam brush. Lay the white tissue paper over the sheet. Apply another coat of glue to the entire surface of the sheet. Let dry.
10: Roll the plastic sheet into a cylinder, overlapping ends about ½"; secure the seam with tacky glue and staple the top and bottom of the seam.
11: Cut a piece of decorative trim to fit around the top of the cylinder and glue in place with tacky glue. ✤

Beaded Evening Bag

Continued from page 67

(*see illustration No. 4 on page 67*);

B: Thread on five silver beads, skip the next black bead on the last strand made and run the needle through the next black bead;

C: Thread on five silver beads, skip the next black bead on the first strand and run the needle through the next black bead;

D: Repeat steps B and C alternately, ending with the top black bead on the first strand (*see illustration No. 4*), then thread on one more silver bead (*this is a **point bead***) and run the needle back through the last black bead.

E: Secure the thread and hide the end. Cut off any extra thread.

8: Thread the beading needle with about 24" of beading thread. Pour 4 mm black faceted round beads into a separate compartment in the bead sorting tray.

9: To **close the bottom,** run the needle through several beads and come out at a point bead (*see illustration No. 5*), fold the Beaded Cover in half with this point bead at the lower right corner.

10: Thread on a silver seed bead, a 4 mm black faceted bead, and a silver seed bead, then run the needle through the next point bead (*see illustration No. 5*). Repeat this sequence until you have joined 19 points.

For the corner, thread on a 4 mm black faceted bead and a silver seed bead; run the needle back through the last black bead (*see illustration No. 6*).

11: Run the needle through the next (20th) point bead (*see blue lines on illustration No. 7*), thread on a silver seed bead and run the needle back through the next 4 mm black faceted bead.

12: Thread on a silver seed bead, run the needle through the next free point bead and thread on a silver seed bead, then run the needle back through the next 4 mm black faceted bead (*see red lines on illustration No. 7*). Repeat this sequence until you have connected all the black faceted beads; thread on a silver seed bead and run the needle through the last remaining point bead.

13: Thread on a 4 mm black faceted bead and a silver seed bead, then run the needle back through the black bead (*same as illustration No. 6*); this is the other corner. Secure, hide and cut the thread.

14: For the **Beaded Fringe,** pour the remaining beads into separate compartments in the bead sorting tray. Thread the beading needle with about 1½ yds. of beading thread, then run the needle through several beads and come out at the second 4 mm black faceted bead from the corner (*see red arrow at top of illustration No. 8*).

15: Thread on two silver seed beads, a black seed bead and two silver seed beads, then thread on the remaining beads (*see red arrows on illustration No. 8*), skip the silver seed bead at the end and go back through the beads in the opposite direction, ending with the black E bead, then thread on two silver seed beads, a black seed bead and two silver seed beads (*see blue lines on illustration No. 8*); go back through the same 4 mm black faceted bead, then through the next three silver seed beads and the next 4 mm black faceted bead.

16: Repeat step 15 until 18 black faceted beads have a Beaded Fringe attached. Secure and hide the thread end. Lay the Beaded Cover aside.

Fabric Bag

1: Allowing ¼" for seams throughout, pin the two lining fabric pieces right sides together and sew along three sides, leaving one 7½" edge open.

2: Pin the two satin fabric pieces right sides together. On each long side, place a pin 2" down from the corner that will be the top (*see Satin Fabric illustration*); sew together across the remainder of the three sides leaving one short edge and 2" at top of each long edge open.

3: On the **sides above the seam,** fold each raw edge ¼" to the wrong side and sew in place.

4: Press the **top raw edge** ½" to the wrong side. Turn right sides out.

5: With wrong sides together, place the lining inside the satin; tack the bottom corners together.

6: On **each side,** with all layers smooth and flat, matching the seams, fold the top pressed edge of the satin to the inside covering the top raw edge of the lining and pin in place; topstitch through all layers close to the pressed edge of the satin.

7: For the **casing,** on each side, sew the satin together ½" below the top folded edge; the area between this seam and the topstitching is the casing.

8: For the **drawstrings,** cut the twisted satin cord in half.

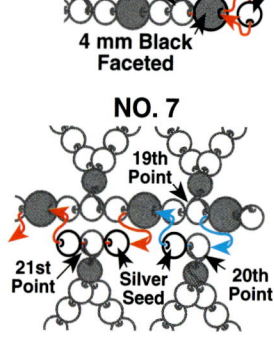

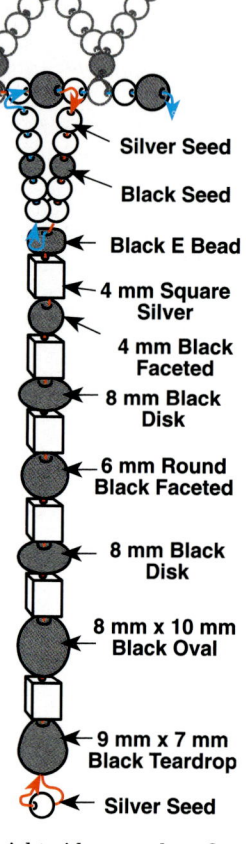

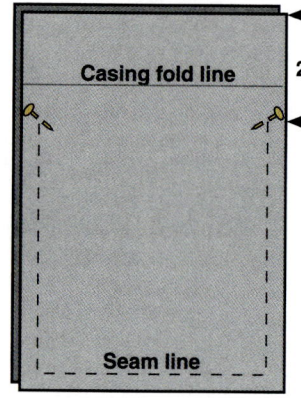

Using the bodkin or safety pin, run one piece of cord through each casing. Tie the two pieces of cord together about 2" from one end and fray the raw ends to resemble a tassel; tie and fray the other end in the same manner.

9: Thread a needle with about 36" of beading thread and pull so both ends are even; hide and secure the thread ends in the knot at one end of the drawstring. String on silver seed beads and wrap the bead strand around both drawstring cords for ½" next to the knot (see photo); secure the thread ends and hide on the inside. Repeat on the other ends of the satin cords.

10: Slip the Beaded Cover over the Fabric Bag. Spacing the remaining point beads evenly around, sew the point beads to the top of the bag catching only the outer layer of the casing.

Five Golden Rings Table Wreath
Continued from page 69

of glue between the base and the greenery at both narrow ends *(do not apply glue near the center where the heart will be attached)*; press together.

7: Apply a generous amount of glue around the bottom of each dowel at the bottom of the heart, center the heart over the base and push the dowels into the base. Let dry.

8: Bend the stems of the pine swag back in place to flow naturally toward the table.

Note: When attaching the ivy vines, pine sprigs and berry clusters to the foam block, use the wire cutters to trim the wire ends to about 1½" long; apply glue to the wire end and insert the wire as far as it will go into the base.

9: To conceal the base, matching the natural flow of the stems on the pine swag, glue the remaining 4" pine sprigs around all four sides and on top of the base.

10: Glue two 14" ivy vines to each short side of the base to extend the overall length of the swag.

11: Working both long sides of the base the same, glue one 6" vine at the center of each long side; glue two 9" vines to the left of the 6" vines and two to the right of the 6" vines.

12: Working from the center top of the heart to the base, securing the ends of the vines with floral pins as you go, wrap four of the 14" vines in a spiral around each side of the heart.

13: In the same manner, fill in the front, center and outside edges of the heart with the remaining 6" and 9" vines.

14: Working both sides the same, glue or pin berry clusters randomly to the front and sides of the heart and to the base, balancing their placement (see photo).

15: Cut the wire-edge ribbon into two 36" lengths. Cut the chenille stem into two 6" pieces.

16: With each length of ribbon, fold a 7"-wide three-loop bow leaving 6" ends for streamers; tightly wrap the center of the bow with one 6" piece of chenille stem and twist to secure. Trim the end of each streamer into a V.

17: Glue one bow to base of the heart on each side.

18: Using a generous amount of glue, attach the cherubs to the center top of the heart on each side (see photo).

19: Thread the five gold rings onto the ⅝" gold ribbon; glue or pin the ribbon ends to hang from the inside top of the heart to the desired length. Trim off any excess ribbon.

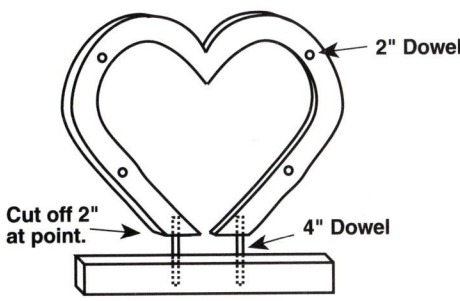

✦ Symbols of Christmas – Candy Cane

A candy maker in Indiana wanted to make a candy that would be a witness, so he made the Christmas Candy Cane. He incorporated several symbols for the birth, ministry and death of Jesus Christ.

He began with a stick of pure white hard candy — white to symbolize the Virgin Birth and the sinless nature of Jesus, and hard to symbolize the Solid Rock, the foundation of the Church and firmness of the promises of God.

The candy maker made the candy in the form of a "J" to represent the name of Jesus. It could also represent the staff of the "Good Shepherd."

Thinking that the candy was somewhat plain, the candy maker stained it with red stripes. He used three small stripes to show the stripes of the scourging Jesus received. The large red stripe represented the blood shed by Christ.

Through time the candy has since become known as a candy cane — a significant decoration seen at Christmas time. Candy canes are not only a holiday treat but are also used to adorn the Christmas tree and other holiday and package decorations.

Peppermint Candy Boxes

Designed by Kenna Prior

Finished Size:
Each box is 1⅜" high × 2" across.

Materials for One:
- 2"-diameter round paper mache box
- Americana® Acrylic Paints by DecoArt™:
  Santa Red #DA170
  White Wash #DA02
- Americana® Gloss Sealer/Finisher #DAS12 by DecoArt™
- Brushes by Loew-Cornell®:
  ¼" Wash Series 7550
  #2 Liner Series 7050
- Clear cellophane gift wrap
- Disposable paint palette or foam plate
- Graphite transfer paper
- Tracing paper
- Pencil
- Peppermint candy

Instructions

1: Remove the lid from the box. With the wash brush and white wash color, paint a base coat on all outer surfaces of the box and the lid. Let dry completely and apply a second coat.
2: For easier handling, cut a 3" × 3" piece of graphite paper and of tracing paper.
3: To transfer the candy swirl pattern to the box lid, trace the Lid pattern on a small piece of tracing paper. Center a piece of graphite paper facedown on the box lid. Center the traced pattern over the graphite paper. Carefully holding the papers in place, trace over the pattern lines, pressing firmly to transfer the design. Remove the papers.
4: To continue the pattern, draw a straight line down from each line of the swirl pattern across the side of the lid to the bottom edge.
5: To transfer the candy swirl pattern to the bottom of the box, trace the Bottom pattern on a piece of tracing paper. Center the graphite paper facedown on the box bottom; center the traced pattern over the graphite paper. Carefully holding the papers in place, trace over the pattern lines. Remove the papers and draw a straight line from each line of the swirl pattern across the side of the box to the top edge.
6: With the wash brush and red, using the pattern lines as guides, paint the swirls on the top and bottom of the box, starting at the edge of the box and curving long brush strokes in toward the center. Let dry.
7: With the same brush, paint the stripes along the side of the box and the box lid. Let dry.
8: To create the highlights on the box lid, thin the white wash with a small amount of water. With the liner brush and thinned white wash, paint a half circle across the box lid about ¼" from the edge *(see photo)*. Let dry.
9: Lay the boxes and lids out on the work surface and spray each with a thin coat of sealer. Let dry.
10: Fill each box with four or five peppermints; matching the red stripes, place the lid on the box.
11: Cut the cellophane into 8" squares. Wrap the box with the cellophane and twist the ends like a piece of candy.
12: Display the Boxes in a candy dish.

LID

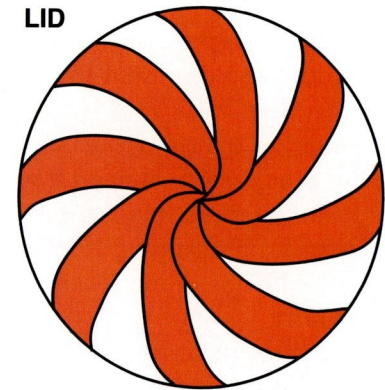

BOTTOM

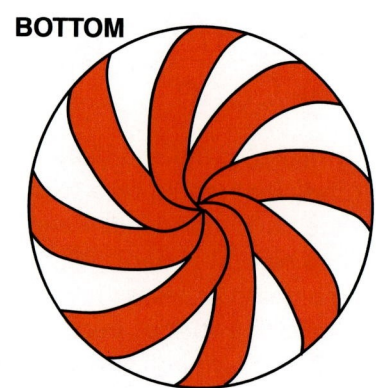

CHAPTER THREE
Gifts Galore

For generations, the holidays have been a time for wishing glad tidings to one and all. We wrap and adorn presents to give as tokens of love, and pause to remember the true meaning of the season.

Clay Bible Cover

Designed by Kenna Prior

Finished Size:
Each Cover is about 4¾" x 7¾".

Materials:
- Products by Amaco®:
    Black #9 Fimo® Polymer Clay *(you will need about 2 oz. for each Cover)*
    Eberhard Faber Fimo® Gold Powder #8709 IN
    Eberhard Faber Fimo® Matte Finish #8706 US
- Mineral oil
- Black Bible *(5½" x 8¼" or size desired)*
- ½" Wash Brush Series 7550 by Loew-Cornell®
- "Count Your Blessings" Book Rubber Stamp Set #780.05 by Rubber Stampede
- Rolling pin or large smooth glass bottle
- Old cookie sheet
- Craft knife or old kitchen knife
- Wax paper
- Aluminum foil
- Fabri-Tac™ by Beacon™ or fabric glue
- Food processor *(optional)*

Note:
Any utensils used for working with the clay should not be used again for food preparation.

Softening the Clay
Method 1: The warmth of your hands will soften the clay by kneading. Work the clay until soft and pliable. Add a drop or two of mineral oil if needed.
Method 2: Break the clay into small pieces and place them in the food processor; add a drop or two of mineral oil and process the clay until a ball is formed.

Instructions
1: After softening the clay by one of the methods listed above, place the clay on a wax paper-covered work surface. Using the rolling pin or a glass bottle, roll out the clay to a thickness of about ¼". For each Bible Cover *(front or back)*, using the knife, cut a clay rectangle to measure ¼" shorter than the Bible on all sides.
2: With your fingers, rub two or three drops of oil over the surface and around the sides of the clay to smooth it out.
3: To prevent the rubber stamps from sticking to the clay, pour a drop or two of oil on the surface of the clay where you intend to stamp; press the stamp down firmly and lift straight up. In this manner, stamp both Covers as shown in the photo or as desired.

Note: Before opening the gold powder, keep in mind that it is very lightweight and, if handled improperly, could become airborne and be inhaled.

4: Cover the top of the powder container with your fingertip and lightly shake the container to coat your fingertip with the powder. To apply the gold powder, lightly dab your fingertip on the raised portions of the clay, not into the crevices of the stamping. Repeat this process until the entire surface has been covered with the gold powder.
5: To create a baking tent for the clay, place a large sheet of foil on the cookie sheet and place the clay in the center. Gather the ends of the foil over the top of the clay and pinch or fold them together to make a tent.
6: Preheat the oven to 275°. Place the cookie sheet in the oven and bake for 25 to 30 minutes. Remove the cookie sheet from the oven and allow the clay to cool partially before removing it from the foil.
7: When the clay is completely cooled, apply a coat of varnish to the top and sides of each Cover with the wash brush; let dry.
8: Apply an even coat of glue to the back of each Cover; place one Cover centered on the front and one Cover centered on the back of the Bible.

❧ Gift Wrapping

Add the ultimate personal touch to your gifts by designing your own wrapping paper. Start with any plain paper such as brown package paper, white glazed paper or plain gift wrapping paper. Then sprinkle it with your own grace notes of glitter, sequins, ribbon rosebuds or paint-stamped motifs. Add fun bows and charming trims.

Sparkly Poinsettia
Materials:
Gift wrapped with white glazed paper
2"-wide red grosgrain ribbon
Gold glitter paint
1"-wide gold ribbon

Instructions:
Make a looped bow with gold ribbon. Attach two streamers of gold ribbon to top center of package; glue bow over top of streamers. Trim streamer ends.

To make poinsettia, cut five 6" lengths of red ribbon. Cut ends diagonally. Hold ribbons together and pinch center. Wrap wire tightly around center and twist wire ends. Attach poinsettia to package. Apply dots of glitter paint to cover wire and form center of poinsettia.

Gift Tubes and Jewelry

Designed by Marilyn Shelton

Gift Tubes

Finished Sizes:
Make each to fit desired gift.

Materials for One of Each:
- Cardboard tubes from bath tissue, paper towels or gift wrap
- Sheet of Gold Corobuff® Metallic Corrugated Paper #7151-0 by Bemiss-Jason Corp.
- Sheet of Spectra™ Multicultural Art Tissue™ #58590 by Bemiss-Jason Corp.
- Sheet of green cellophane
- Scrap pieces of solid color and Christmas-print wrapping paper
- 1½"-wide red silk poinsettia
- 2 yds. ⅛"-wide red ribbon with gold edge
- Sheet of red tissue paper
- 14" piece of 1½"-wide Christmas ribbon
- 1½ yds. of ½"-wide mesh ribbon
- 2 gold 1" ribbon roses
- Gold cord
- Scissors
- Adhesives by Therm O Web:
    PeelnStick™ ¼" Double-Sided Tape #3749
    Keep a Memory™ Sticky Dots #4051
- Crafty® Magic Melt® Oval Magic Pro Glue Gun by Adhesive Technologies, Inc.
- Crafty® Magic Melt® Glue Sticks by Adhesive Technologies, Inc.

Santa Tube

1: Cut the gold corrugated paper to the size needed to wrap around the gift, allowing an extra ½" in width for overlapping. Following the manufacturer's instructions, apply a piece of tape down one long edge; roll the paper into a tube, overlap ½" and secure with the tape.

2: Place the gift centered on one short end of the sheet of red tissue paper, roll the gift in the tissue and secure with a small piece of tape. Insert the paper and gift into the corrugated tube *(see photo)*.

3: Cut two 10" pieces from the red ribbon; cut the remaining ribbon in half. Tie one 10" piece of ribbon tightly around each end of the tissue paper leaving the long ends for streamers. On each end, fold one long piece of ribbon into a multi-looped bow and use the long streamers to tie it to the end of the gift.

4: Cut a Santa face or other design from a scrap of Christmas-print wrapping paper. Following the manufac-

Continued on page 93

Cookie Food Gifts

Designed by Marilyn Shelton

Snowman Cookie Jar

Finished Size:
Jar shown is 7¾" tall.

Materials for Jar:
- One-quart snowman-shaped jar or other desired one-quart container
- Air-Dry PermEnamel™ Surface Conditioner by Delta Technical Coatings
- Air-Dry PermEnamel™ Gel Glass Paints™ by Delta Technical Coatings:
    - Blue #45 740
    - Orange #45 738
    - Red #45 750
- 16" piece of 1"-wide Black Taffeta Ribbon by Offray
- ⅞"-long Green Lacquered Holly Leaves with Berries #02001 by Darice®
- 18" piece of Gold Cord by Offray
- Old Christmas card
- Small round paintbrush
- Crafty® Magic Melt® Floral Pro™ Glue Gun by Adhesive Technologies, Inc.
- Crafty® Magic Melt® Glue Sticks by Adhesive Technologies, Inc.

Instructions
1: Clean and dry the jar thoroughly, inside and out.
2: Following the manufacturer's instructions, prepare the jar's outer surface with the conditioner.
3: Following the manufacturer's instructions, with the small paintbrush and glass paint, paint the accents on the snowman as desired; let dry.
4: For the **hatband,** cut a piece of ribbon to fit around the hat plus ½" for overlap; glue the ribbon in place overlapping the ends ½".
5: For the **bow,** cut a 5" piece of ribbon; fold the ribbon in half with the ends overlapping ¼" at the center, glue the bow to the hatband covering the seam.
6: For the **center** of the bow, fold the remaining piece of ribbon into a tube and secure with a drop of glue; glue this to the center of the bow.
7: To make the **recipe card** *(see Oatmeal Raisin Cookie Recipe),* use the front cover or cut the design from an old Christmas card *(make sure the back side has no writing on it);* write the cookie recipe on the back of the card.
8: Punch a small hole in the card on one side *(do not punch through the recipe)* and attach the card to the jar with gold cord.

Filling the Jar
Note: The Cookie Jar is filled with the dry ingredients and raisins from the recipe. The gift recipient will need to provide the vegetable oil and eggs.
1: In a large bowl, combine flour, baking powder and salt; mix well. Spoon the flour mixture into the jar for the first layer.
2: Next, add a layer of oats, a layer of white sugar, a layer of brown sugar and a layer of coconut.
3: Remove the plastic cover from the jar lid and fill the lid with the raisins. Replace the plastic cover, place the lid on the jar. If your jar does not have a hollow lid, layer the raisins on top of the coconut.

Oatmeal Raisin Cookie Recipe
1¼ cups flour
1 cup quick oats
1 cup coconut
½ cup brown sugar
½ cup white sugar
½ cup raisins
½ tsp. baking powder
¼ teaspoon salt
⅓ cup vegetable oil
2 eggs

Preheat oven to 350°. In a large bowl, place the dry ingredients and raisins *(from the cookie jar);* mix well. In a separate bowl, beat together vegetable oil and eggs; add to dry ingredients. Stir until mixture forms a soft dough. Drop dough by teaspoonfuls onto a greased cookie sheet and bake 8 to 10 minutes.

Doily Cookie Jar

Finished Size:
Jar shown is 7" tall.

Materials for Jar:
- One-quart mason jar or other desired one-quart container with lid
- 10"-round White and Ecru Crochet Doily by Wimpole Street
- 2½ yds. of ⅛"-wide Red ribbon with Gold Metallic Edge by Offray
- 2 Gold ¾" Jingle Bells #1090-05 by Darice®
- Old Christmas card
- Small plastic zipper bag

Instructions
Note: The Cookie Jar is filled with the dry ingredients from the recipe. The gift recipient will need to provide the butter, milk, vanilla and peanut butter.
1: Clean and dry the jar thoroughly, inside and out.
2: Spoon the sugar into the jar; layer the cocoa on top of the sugar.
3: To keep the oats separate from the other ingredients, place them in a small zipper bag; lay the bag on top of the cocoa as the last layer.

Continued on page 94

Christmas Greeting Cards

Designed by Kathy Wegner

St. Nick With Snowflakes

Finished Size:
5" x 6½".

Materials for One:
- 5" x 6½" blank greeting card with envelope
- 2¾" x 5¾" St. Nick print *(purchased or cut from old card)*
- ½" x 1⅜" "Merry Christmas" print *(purchased or cut from old card)*
- Tan parchment print cardstock:
    - 1" x 2" piece
    - 5" x 6½" piece
- 4" x 6½" piece of green paper
- Snowflake Rubber Stamp #665D by All Night Media
- Topaz and metallic copper pigment ink pads
- 8½" x 11" sheet of Keep a Memory™ Acid-Free Mounting Adhesive #3821 by Therm O Web
- Stamp Edge Paper Edgers by Fiskars®
- 28" piece of red metallic floss
- 1"-wide foam tape
- 2 small bay leaves *(or other dried leaves)*
- Small sponge
- Old newspaper
- Ruler
- Scissors
- Craft glue

Instructions
1: Following the manufacturer's instructions, apply the mounting adhesive to the back of the St. Nick and Merry Christmas prints, the green paper and the 5" x 6½" parchment paper.
2: With scissors, if needed, cut out the St. Nick and Merry Christmas designs *(see photo)*.
3: To give the prints an antique look, press the tip of the sponge on the topaz ink pad and rub the ink lightly on the edges and white areas of both prints.
4: Remove the release paper from the back of the St. Nick design and adhere it centered on the green paper. Using the paper edgers, trim the green paper around St. Nick leaving a ¼" border all around.
5: Remove the release paper from the Merry Christmas print; adhere it centered on the 1" x 2" piece of cardstock. Trim the cardstock edges with the paper edgers leaving a 1/16" border all around.
6: Using the snowflake stamp and copper ink, randomly stamp snowflakes on the 5" x 6½" piece of cardstock. Let dry.
7: To guild the edges of the green paper, place the green paper on old newspaper, press the tip of the sponge on the copper ink pad and dab the ink over ⅛" on the cut edges of the green paper *(see photo)*.
8: In the same manner, guild the cut edges of the Merry Christmas print.
9: Remove the release paper from the 5" x 6½" piece of cardstock; adhere it centered on the front of the card. Remove the release paper from the green paper and adhere it centered over the cardstock.
10: Using a ½" x 1" piece of foam tape, adhere the Merry Christmas print to the greeting card.
11: Glue the two dried leaves to the bottom of the Merry Christmas print with craft glue, tucking stems underneath.
12: Cut four 7" pieces of metallic floss; holding the pieces together, tie in a small bow, glue over the leaves at bottom of the Merry Christmas print.

Angel With Letter

Finished Size:
5" x 6½".

Materials for One:
- 5" x 6½" blank ivory greeting card with envelope
- 2¾" x 4½" angel print *(purchased or cut from old card)*
- 4½" x 6½" piece of ivory cardstock
- 4" x 5½" piece of blue paper
- Scraps of blue paper for punching
- Keep a Memory™ Acid-Free products by Therm O Web:
    - 8½" x 11" sheet of Mounting Adhesive #3821
    - Sticky Dots Adhesive #4051
- Desired Paper Edgers by Fiskars®
- Rubber stamp with "handwritten letter" design *(4" x 5½" or larger)*
- Topaz and sky gray pigment inking pads
- Angel Frame Punch by McGill®
- 20" of 18 mm blue organza ribbon
- Small sponge
- Scissors
- Ruler

Instructions
1: Using the rubber stamp and sky gray ink, stamp the 4½" x 6½" piece of cardstock one time; without re-inking, move the stamp over to one side and down about ¼" and stamp the cardstock again.
2: With paper edgers, trim the letter-stamped cardstock to 4" x 5½".
3: To give the letter an antique appearance, press your fingertip on the topaz ink pad and gently rub it between the stamped areas and along the cut edges of the letter. Press the tip of the sponge on the sky gray ink pad and randomly dab it lightly around the edges of the letter.
4: Leaving a 4" tail on one side, tie the ribbon in a 2" single-

Continued on page 92

Christmas Greeting Cards
Continued from page 91

loop bow and attach the bow to the top of the letter with a sticky dot *(see photo)*. Wrap the 4" tail to the back of the card; wrap the remaining long end of ribbon around the back of the card and across the front as shown in photo. Adhere both ribbon ends with sticky dots.

5: Adhere the letter to the front of the card with five or six sticky dots.
6: Following the manufacturer's instructions, apply the mounting adhesive to the backs of the angel and the blue paper.
7: With scissors, cut out the angel design; remove the backing paper from the angel and adhere it centered on the blue paper.
8: With decorative scissors, trim the blue paper around the angel design leaving a ¼" to ½" border all around *(see photo)*.
9: Remove the backing paper from the blue paper and adhere the angel design to the front of the greeting card at a slight angle.
10: Using the angel punch, punch two angels from the blue paper and adhere them to the front of the card with sticky dots.

Musician Angels

Finished Size:
5" x 6½".

Materials for One:
- ❏ 4" x 5½" blank ivory greeting card with envelope
- ❏ 2 copies of 2½" x 3½" Angel print *(purchased or cut from old card)*
- ❏ 4" x 5" piece of ivory cardstock
- ❏ 3½'" x 4½" piece of plaid paper to match angel print
- ❏ 5½" piece of 1⅜"-wide print ribbon to match angel print *(musical note ribbon is shown)*
- ❏ Keep a Memory™ Acid-Free Sticky Dots Adhesive #4051 by Therm O Web
- ❏ Ripple Edge Paper Edgers by Fiskars®
- ❏ Turquoise and metallic gold pigment ink pads or colors to match angel print
- ❏ 1"-wide foam tape
- ❏ Small sponge
- ❏ Scissors
- ❏ Ruler

Instructions
1: Press your fingertip on the gold ink pad and smear a faint oval frame of gold around the front edges of the greeting card; press the sponge on the gold ink pad and dab highlights around the frame. With the same sponge, dab turquoise ink around the frame of the card.
2: If desired, dab small amounts of matching-color ink onto the ribbon.
3: Following the manufacturer's instructions, apply sticky dots to the edges of the ribbon and vertically attach the ribbon to the center front of the card *(see photo)*.
4: Using scissors, cut the design from one angel print. Cut a ½" x 1" piece of foam tape and adhere it to the back of the cutout design. Matching the outlines of both prints, place the cutout design directly on top of the design on the second print.
5: With scissors, cut a 2¼" x 3¼" oval from the second angel print *(see photo)*.
6: With the paper edgers, cut a 2½" x 3¾" oval from the plaid paper. Cut a 1" x 2½" piece of foam tape and adhere the oval angel print centered on the plaid oval.
7: Adhere the angel design to the center of the greeting card with sticky dots.

Woodsy St. Nick

Finished Size:
4" x 5½".

Materials for One:
- ❏ 4" x 5½" Corrugated Kraft Card with Envelope from The Paper Reflections Line by DMD Industries, Inc.
- ❏ 2" x 3¼" St. Nick print *(purchased or cut from old card)*
- ❏ 2¼" x 3½" piece of white cardstock
- ❏ 3" x 4½" piece of green tissue paper
- ❏ 3½" x 5½" piece of tree-print paper
- ❏ 8½" x 11" sheet of Keep a Memory™ Acid-Free Mounting Adhesive #3821 by Therm O Web
- ❏ Deckle Edge Paper Edgers by Fiskars®
- ❏ 1"-wide foam tape
- ❏ Scissors
- ❏ Ruler

Instructions
1: Following the manufacturer's instructions, apply the mounting adhesive to the back of the St. Nick print, the tissue paper and the tree-print paper.
2: Remove the release paper from the back of the St. Nick print and adhere the print centered on the cardstock. With scissors, cut out the St. Nick design *(see photo)*.
3: While holding the St. Nick design centered over the green tissue, use the paper edgers to cut the green tissue around St. Nick leaving a ½" to ¾" border all around *(see photo)*.
4: Remove the release paper from the green tissue, center the tissue on the tree-print paper. In the same manner as before, leaving a ¼" border of the green tissue all around, cut out the tree-print with the paper edgers.
5: Remove the release paper from the tree-print and adhere it centered on front of the corrugated card.
6: Cut three pieces of foam tape each ½" x 1". Remove the backing from the tape and apply the pieces of tape evenly spaced across the back of the St. Nick design; adhere the design centered on the front of the card. ❦

Gift Tubes and Jewelry

Continued from page 87

turer's instructions, apply the design to the tube with sticky dots.

Angel Tube

1: Cut a cardboard tube to the size needed for the desired gift. Cut a piece of art tissue 8" longer than the tube and wide enough to fit around the tube with ½" extra for overlapping.

2: With the tissue laying face down on the work surface, fold each end down 2" and tape in place, forming a piece 4" longer than the tube.

3: Place the cardboard tube centered along one unfolded edge on the wrong side of the tissue, tape the unfolded edge of the tissue to the tube, roll the tissue around the tube and tape the other unfolded edge in place.

4: Cut two 8" pieces from the mesh ribbon; wrap one piece around the tissue at one end of the tube and tie a knot *(see photo)* leaving the long ends for streamers. Place the gift inside the tube and tie the remaining 8" ribbon on the opposite end to seal the tube.

5: Cut the remaining length of mesh ribbon in half and fold each piece into a 6"-wide bow, tie to the tube with the long streamers. Trim ends as desired.

6: Using hot glue, attach a gold ribbon rose to the center of each bow.

7: Cut an angel or other design from a scrap of Christmas-print wrapping paper and apply to the tube with sticky dots.

Poinsettia Tube

1: Cut a cardboard tube to fit the desired gift. Cut a piece of solid color wrapping paper *(gold is shown in photo)* 2" longer than the tube and wide enough to fit around the tube with ½" extra for overlapping.

2: Place the tube centered along one edge on the wrong side of the wrapping paper, tape the edge of the paper to the tube, roll the paper around the tube and tape the other edge in place. Tuck the ends of the paper inside the tube.

3: Cut two pieces of 1½"-wide Christmas ribbon to fit around the tube plus ½" for overlapping. Wrap one piece of ribbon around one end of the tube *(see photo)* and secure with hot glue; repeat with the other piece of ribbon on the other end of the tube.

4: With hot glue, attach the poinsettia centered on one side of the tube.

5: Cut a piece of cellophane wide enough to wrap around the gift several times and 8" longer than the tube. Place the gift centered on the cellophane, roll the cellophane around the gift and secure the edge of the cellophane with tape.

6: With the gold cord, tie a bow around each end of the cellophane. Insert the wrapped gift into the tube *(see photo)*.

Charm Bracelet & Earrings

Finished Sizes:

Bracelet is 8" long. Earrings are 1¼" long.

Materials:

❑ Charms and Bracelet by Creative Beginnings:
  7¼"-long Gold Bracelet #2619
  24K Gold Plated Christmas Theme
  Charm Pack #CF590829
  2 Gold ¾" Snowflake Charms #2951
❑ 2 gold kidney-shaped pierced earring wires
❑ 7 small gold jump rings
❑ Jewelry pliers or needle nose pliers

Instructions

1: Using the pliers to separate the jump rings, attach the Christmas charms with jump rings evenly spaced across the bracelet.

2: Slide each snowflake charm onto one earring wire.

Jingle Bell Necklace & Earrings

Finished Size:

Necklace is 16" long. Earrings are 1" long.

Materials:

❑ 30" of Burgundy Twisted Cord by Wrights®
❑ Gold Jingle Bells by Darice®:
  Large #1090-07 *(1")*
  2 Small #1090-03 *(½")*
❑ 2 gold kidney-shaped pierced earring wires
❑ Large gold jump ring
❑ 2 small gold jump rings
❑ Jewelry pliers or needle nose pliers
❑ Permanent No Fray by Ridlen Adhesives

Instructions

1: Apply No Fray to each cut end of the cord and let dry.

2: With the pliers, separate the large jump ring, place the large jingle bell on the ring and reclose. In the same manner, attach a small jump ring to each of the small jingle bells.

3: For the **necklace,** thread the cord through the large jump ring on the large jingle bell; tie the ends of the cord in a knot.

4: For the **earrings,** place one small jingle bell on each earring wire.

Beaded Necklace

Finished Size:

15" long, including charms.

Materials:

❑ 29" piece of red 1/16" cord
❑ 6 wooden 8 mm beads
❑ 28 wooden 6 mm beads
❑ 8 assorted ½" to 1" resin Christmas figurines with holes through the center *(Christmas beads)*
❑ 1½" Christmas charm with ring
❑ Fabric glue

Instructions

1: String three sets of beads and the Christmas charm onto the red cord as follows:
  A: String on a Christmas bead, two 6 mm beads, one 8 mm bead, two 6 mm beads.
  B: Repeat step A two more times, then string on another Christmas bead.
  C: String on two 6 mm beads, the Christmas charm and

Continued on page 94

Gift Tubes and Jewelry
Continued from page 93

two 6 mm beads *(this is the center section)*.
  D: Repeat steps A and B. Tie the ends of the cord together.
2: To keep the spacing between the beads and the charms, lay the necklace out on a flat work surface and find the center of the cord; position the Christmas charm at the center of the cord. Working outward from the center, evenly space the beads and charms along the cord.
3: Being careful not to move the position of the charms and beads, place a small dot of glue on each side of each charm and each bead to hold it in place. Let the glue dry thoroughly.

Cookie Food Gifts
Continued from page 88

4: Replace the jar lid on top of the jar.
5: Cut a 23" piece of ribbon. Place the doily centered over the top of the jar lid; tie the ribbon around the top of the jar to secure *(see photo)*, leaving the long streamers.
6: Cut a 10" piece of ribbon and set aside. Tie the remaining ribbon into a 5"-wide multi-looped bow and secure the center of the bow with the 10" piece of ribbon.
7: Attach a jingle bell to each end of the 10" ribbon.
8: To make the **recipe card,** use the front cover or cut the design from an old Christmas card *(make sure the back side has no writing on it)*; write the No-Bake Cookie Recipe on the back.
9: Punch a small hole in the card *(do not punch through the recipe)*. Thread one long streamer from the jar ribbon through the hole in the recipe card; holding the bow and the recipe card up against the jar, use the long streamers from the jar ribbon to tie around the bow.

No-Bake Cookie Recipe
3 cups quick oats
2 cups sugar
¼ cup cocoa
1 stick butter or margarine
½ cup milk
½ cup peanut butter
1 tablespoon of vanilla

Combine sugar, cocoa, butter and milk in a medium saucepan. Bring to a boil over medium heat and boil for one minute. In a large mixing bowl, combine peanut butter, oats and vanilla. Stir in cocoa mixture and mix well. Drop by teaspoonfuls onto foil; let cool.

How To Say Merry Christmas in Many Languages

Arabic—I'd Miilad Said Oua Sana Saida
Bohemian—Vesele Vanoce
Brazilian—Boas Festas e Feliz Ano Novo
Danish—Gloedelig Jul
English—Merry Christmas
Estonian—Ruumsaid juulup\hi
Finnish—Hyvaa joulua
French—Joyeux Noel
German—Froehliche Weihnachten
Greek—Kala Christouyenna!
Hawaiian—Mele Kalikimaka
Hebrew—Mo'adim Lesimkha. Chena tova
Hindi—Shub Naya Baras
Hungarian—Kellemes Karacsonyi unnepeket
Icelandic—Gledileg Jol
Indonesian—Selamat Hari Natal
Iraqi—Idah Saidan Wa Sanah Jadidah
Irish—Nollaig Shona Dhuit
Italian—Buone Feste Natalizie
Korean—Sung Tan Chuk Ha
Lithuanian—Linksmu Kaledu
Manx—Nollick ghennal as blein vie noa
Maori—Meri Kirihimete
Marathi—Shub Naya Varsh
Navajo—Merry Keshmish
Norwegian—God Jul
Polish—Wesolych Swiat Bozego Narodzenia
Portuguese—Boan Festas
Rumanian—Sarbaori vesele}
Serbian—Hristos se rodi
Slovakian—Sretan Bozic or Vesele Vianoce
Sami—Buorrit Juovllat
Scots Gaelic—Nollaig chridheil huibh
Slovak—Vesele Vianoce. A stastlivy Novy Rok
Slovene—Vesele Bozicne. Screcno Novo Leto
Spanish—Feliz Navidad
Swedish—God Jul and (Och) Ett Gott Nytt Ar
Tamil—Nathar Puthu Varuda Valthukkal
Thai—Sawadee Pee Mai
Turkish—Noeliniz Ve Yeni Yiliniz Kutlu Olsun
Ukrainian—Srozhdestvom Kristovym
Vietnamese—Chung Mung Giang Sinh
Yugoslavian—Cestitamo Bozic

Old-World Santa Pin

Designed by Cheryl Gutierrez

Finished Size:
About 3¼" tall.

Materials:
- ❏ Sculpey III® Polymer Clay by Polyform®
- ❏ Apple Barrel Colors® Acrylic Paint by Plaid®:
    Tapestry Wine #20592
    Bright Peach #20203
    Black #20504
- ❏ Matte Acrylic Spray Sealer by Krylon®
- ❏ ¼" paintbrush
- ❏ Scuff Magic Brown Shoe Polish *(with sponge applicator)* by Kiwi®
- ❏ 1½" pin back with safety lock
- ❏ Paper towels
- ❏ Toothpicks
- ❏ Cookie sheet
- ❏ Hot glue gun and glue sticks
- ❏ Conventional oven

Instructions
1: Pinch off a 1½" to 2" ball of clay and work it in your hands until soft and smooth; **each piece of clay will be worked in this manner**.
2: Roll the softened clay into a 4" to 4½"-long roll.
3: For Santa's **hat**, shape ¾" at one end of the roll into a point and bend over against the remainder of the roll.
4: For the **body**, using your thumb, press the other end of the roll to about 1" wide and ¼" thick with a fairly squared bottom.
5: For the **beard**, pinch off another 1" ball of clay and shape into a 2"-long roll that is a little wider at the top than at the bottom, then slightly flatten the full length of the roll. Press the wider end across the top of the body just under the tip of the hat. Now gently twist the loose end of the beard to give it that long, old-world look *(see photo)*.
6: For the **robe fur**, pinch off a ¼" ball of clay and roll into a ¾" strip; gently press in place across the bottom of the body.
7: For the **hat fur**, pinch off a ¼" ball of clay and roll into a 1" strip; with the ends at top corners of the beard, shape the strip into a curve to outline the face and press gently in place.
8: Pinch off a ¼" ball of clay and roll into a tiny ball; place it over the point of the hat for a pom-pom.
9: For the **mustache**, pinch off a ½" ball of clay and shape a tapered roll coming to a dull point at each end. Bend at the center and gently press in place at the center top of the beard.
10: To **add texture** to the beard, using long strokes and following the curve of the twists, drag the end of a toothpick across the beard to resemble hair. Add texture to the mustache in the same manner.
11: To **add texture** to the robe and hat fur, drag the end of a toothpick in tiny circles over each section to give it a fluffy look.
12: Place the assembled Santa on the cookie sheet and bake according to the manufacturer's instructions. Different thicknesses of clay require different baking times.
13: When baking is complete, remove from the oven and allow to cool.
14: Using the paintbrush, paint the robe and hat with tapestry wine, paint the face with peach. Let dry.
15: For **eyes**, dip the end of a toothpick into the black paint and make two small dots on the face. Let dry.
16: Using the sponge applicator, dab brown shoe polish over the entire Santa to give him an old, antique look; remove any excess by dabbing with a paper towel. Let dry.
17: Apply a coat of spray sealer to all surfaces of the Santa; let dry. Repeat for a second coat.
18: Glue the pin back to the back of the Santa.

Braided Necklaces

Designed by Minette Collins Smith

Silver Necklace

Finished Size:
20" long; length can be adjusted.

Materials:
- White/Silver #1S Metallic Knit-Cro-Sheen® Art. A64M by J. & P. Coats® or size 10 crochet cotton thread
- Jewelry Findings and Charms by Creative Beginnings:
    Silver Lobster Clasp #2681
    10 Small Silver Jump Rings #2642
    2 Medium Silver Cord Connectors #F-18
    2 Glass Drop with Silver Wrap Fuchsia #5413
    2 Glass Drop with Silver Wrap Emerald #5414
    2 Glass Drop with Silver Wrap Sapphire #5415
    2 Glass Drop with Silver Wrap Lt. Amethyst #5417
- Needle nose pliers
- Ruler or tape measure

Note:
Adjust length by cutting each strand of thread an extra 1" for each 1" of additional length desired.

Instructions
1: Cut 15 strands of white/silver thread each 28" long. Holding all strands together as one, tie a knot 1½" from one end. Tie a knot 5" from the first knot.
2: Separate the threads into three groups with five threads in each group. Braid the three groups until you have a braided section 7" long.
3: Tie a knot at the end of the braided section. Tie another knot 5" from the last knot made.
4: Trim the ends of the thread 1½" from the last knot.
5: With pliers, fasten a cord connector to each end of the necklace, covering the raw ends of the thread. Fasten a jump ring and lobster clasp to one end of the necklace and a jump ring to the opposite end.
6: With pliers, attach a jump ring to each of the eight glass drop charms; use another jump ring to attach each of the charm jump rings to the braided section evenly spaced across 3" at center *(see photo)*.

Snowflake Necklace

Finished Size:
17" long; length can be adjusted.

Materials:
- Gold/Gold #90G Knit-Cro-Sheen® Art. A64M by J. & P. Coats® or size 10 crochet cotton thread
- Gold #5 Metallic #8 Braid by Kreinik Mfg. Co.
- Jewelry Findings and Charms by Creative Beginnings:
    Gold Lobster Clasp #2680
    2 Medium Gold Jump Rings #F-15
    9 Small Gold Jump Rings #2608
    2 Medium Gold Cord Connectors #F-17
    Gold Snowflake #9226 *(1")*
    2 Gold Snowflakes #6039 *(⅞")*
    2 Gold Snowflakes # 9227 *(⅝")*
    2 Gold Snowflakes # 9228 *(½")*
- Needle nose pliers
- Ruler or tape measure

Note:
Adjust length by cutting each strand of thread an extra 1" for each 1" of additional length desired.

Instructions
1: Cut 10 strands of gold/gold thread each 24" long and cut five strands of gold braid each 24" long. Holding all strands together as one, tie a knot 5" from one end.
2: Separate the gold/gold threads into two groups with five threads in each group; separate the gold braid into another group. Braid the three groups until you have a braided section 6" long.
3: Tie a knot at the end of the braided section. Trim threads 5" from last knot made.
4: With pliers, fasten a cord connector to each end of the necklace, covering the raw ends of the thread. Fasten a medium jump ring and lobster clasp to one end of the necklace and a medium jump ring to the opposite end.
5: With pliers, placing the largest snowflake at the center and decreasing sizes so the smallest are at each end, use jump rings to attach the snowflakes evenly spaced across the center 3" of the braided section *(see photo)*.

Fairy Necklace

Finished Size:
18½" long; length can be adjusted.

Materials:
- Ecru/Gold #61G Metallic Knit-Cro-Sheen® Art. A64M by J. & P. Coats® or size 10 crochet cotton thread
- Gold #5 Metallic #8 Braid by Kreinik Mfg. Co.
- Jewelry Findings and Charms by Creative Beginnings:
    Gold Lobster Clasp #2680
    2 Medium Gold Jump Rings #F-15
    2 Small Gold Jump Rings #2608
    2 Medium Gold Cord Connectors #F-17
    Gold Large Fairy #2814 *(1" x 1¾" fairy charm)*
- Needle nose pliers

Continued on page 100

Bottle Gift Bags

Designed by Minette Collins Smith

Finished Size:
Each Bag fits tall, slender wine bottle or similar bottle up to 3½" diameter × 12" high.

Materials for Each:
- Tall, slender bottle of wine or similar beverage (*up to 3½" diameter x 12" high*)
- ½" paintbrush
- Sewing thread to match fabric
- Sewing needle or sewing machine
- Flat paper-covered work surface

Additional Materials for Black With Silver Swirls:
- 10"-wide piece of crisp, sheer black 36"- to 42"-wide fabric with selvage on short ends
- Desired rubber stamp (*shown is a 2½"-wide swirl*)
- Dazzling Metallics™ Shimmering Silver #DA70 Acrylic Paint by DecoArt™
- 30" of decorative silver ½"-wide rope
- 1 yd. of silver medium #16 metallic braid
- 1" silver man-in-the-moon charm

Additional Materials for Tan With Bronze & Gold Leaves:
- 10"-wide piece of crisp, sheer tan 36"- to 42"-wide fabric with selvage on short ends
- Desired rubber stamps (*shown are two 2" x 4" leaves*)
- Dazzling Metallics™ Acrylic Paint by DecoArt™:
    Bronze #DA73
    Venetian Gold #DA72
- 32"-long gold ¼"-wide twisted cord with tassels

Additional Materials for Silver With White Stars:
- 10"-wide piece of crisp, sheer pale gray 36"- to 42"-wide fabric with selvage on short ends
- Desired rubber stamp (*shown is a 3" starburst*)
- Dazzling Metallics™ White Pearl #DA117 Acrylic Paint by DecoArt™
- 1 yd. of white 6 mm strung beads (*or decorative rope, twisted cord, braid, etc.*)
- Hot glue gun and glue sticks

Additional Materials for White With Gold Stars:
- 10"-wide piece of crisp, sheer white 36"- to 42"-wide fabric with selvage on short ends
- Desired rubber stamps (*shown are ⅜" and ½" stars*)
- Dazzling Metallics™ Glorious Gold #DA71 Acrylic Paint by DecoArt™
- 1 yd. of white and gold ⅜" twisted cord
- 1 yd. of gold medium #16 metallic braid
- 2" gold shooting star charm

Continued on page 100

Gifts Galore ~ page 99

Bottle Gift Bags
Continued from page 99

Instructions

1: Spread the fabric right side up on the paper-covered work surface.
2: Following the manufacturer's instructions, for each image, brush the rubber stamp with the desired paint, firmly press the rubber stamp on the fabric where desired. When the fabric is sufficiently covered with the stamped design, let the paint dry.
3: Fold the fabric in half with stamped design on the inside. With the selvage at one short edge, cut two 7½" × 17" pieces from the fabric.
4: Sew the raw edges together on three sides leaving the selvage edge open. Turn right side out.
5: Place the wine bottle inside the bag; tuck the top selvage edge to the inside even with or just below the top of the bottle, or if desired, fold to the outside. Gather the Bag around the neck of the bottle.
6: For the tie on the **black Gift Bag,** tie a knot at each end of the decorative silver rope. Wrap the rope around the neck of the wine bottle to gather the fabric and tie a loose knot to hold.
7: Thread the man-in-the-moon charm onto the silver metallic braid; tie the charm in place at the center. With the charm at front, wrap the braid two times around the gathers of the Gift Bag and tie to hold *(see photo)*.
8: For the tie on the **tan Gift Bag,** wrap the gold cord with tassels around the neck of the wine bottle to gather the fabric and tie a large bow to hold.
9: For the tie on the **silver Gift Bag,** tie the ends of the strung beads together and glue to hold. Wrap the strung beads two times around the neck of the wine bottle to gather the fabric. Tie the remainder of the bead strand in a loose knot to hold *(see photo)*.
10: For the tie on the **white Gift Bag,** wrap the white and gold twisted cord around the neck of the wine bottle to gather the fabric and tie a large bow to hold.
11: Thread the shooting star charm onto the gold metallic thread; tie the charm in place at the center. With the charm at front, wrap the thread two times around the gathers of the Gift Bag and tie to hold *(see photo)*.

Braided Necklaces
Continued from page 96

❏ Ruler or tape measure

Note:
Adjust length by cutting each strand of thread an extra 1" for each 1" of additional length desired.

Instructions

1: Cut 10 strands of ecru/gold thread each 24" long; cut five strands of gold braid each 24" long. Holding all strands together as one, tie a knot 1" from one end. Tie a knot 5" from the first knot.
2: Separate the ecru/gold threads into two groups with five threads in each; separate the gold braid into another group. Braid the three groups until you have a braided section 7" long.
3: Tie a knot at the end of the braided section. Tie another knot 5" from the last knot made.
4: Trim the thread ends 1" from the last knot.
5: With pliers, fasten a cord connector to each end of the necklace, covering the raw ends of the thread. Fasten a medium jump ring and lobster clasp to one end of the necklace and a medium jump ring to the opposite end.
6: With pliers, use two small jump rings to attach the fairy to the center of the braided section.

Heart Necklace

Finished Size:
17½" long; length can be adjusted.

Materials:
❏ Metallic Knit-Cro-Sheen® Art. A64M by J. & P. Coats® or size 10 crochet cotton thread:
    Ecru/Gold #61G
    Gold/Gold #90G
❏ Gold #5 Metallic #8 Braid by Kreinik Mfg. Co.
❏ Jewelry Findings and Charms by Creative Beginnings:
    Gold Lobster Clasp #2680
    11 Large Gold Jump Rings #2623
    5 Medium Gold Jump Rings #F-15
    4 Small Gold Jump Rings #2608
    2 Gold ½" Necklace Clamps #3815
    5 Gold Heart w/Filigrees #1274
    4 Gold Wire Hearts #6022
    4 Gold Rimmed Hearts #6024
❏ 24-gauge gold wire
❏ Needle nose wire cutter pliers
❏ Ruler or tape measure

Note:
Adjust length by cutting each strand of thread an extra 1" for each 1" of additional length desired.

Instructions

1: Cut 30 strands of gold/gold thread each 24" long, cut 18 strands of ecru/gold each 24" long, cut six strands gold braid each 24" long.
2: Holding all strands together as one, tightly wrap the gold wire several times around all strands 2" from one end, covering about ¼". Tie a knot in all strands 6" from the wire.
3: For **braiding,** separate the threads into one group with 18 strands of ecru/gold, a second group with 18 strands of gold/gold and a third group with 12 strands of gold/gold and six strands of gold braid. Braid the three groups of thread until you have a braided section 5" long.
4: Tie a knot at the end of the braided section.
5: Tightly wrap the wire several times around the loose end of the threads 6" from the last knot made, covering about ¼". Trim the thread ends to ¼".
6: At each end of the necklace, with pliers, fasten a cord clamp to the end, covering the raw ends of the thread. Fasten a large jump ring and lobster clasp to one end of the necklace and a large jump ring to the opposite end.

7: With pliers, use medium jump rings to attach each large heart to a large jump ring; attach the large jump rings evenly spaced across the center of the braided section.

8: Use a small jump ring to attach a wire heart and a rimmed heart to each of the last four large jump rings; attach the large jump rings to the braided section centered between large hearts *(see photo)*.

Lightbulb Necklace

Finished Size:
18" long; length can be adjusted.

Materials:
- Needloft® Craft Cord by Uniek, Inc. or metallic craft cord:
    - White/Gold #07
    - Solid Gold #20
- Miniature Christmas lightbulb charms:
    - 8 assorted-color 1"-long
    - 9 assorted-color ½"-long
- Jewelry Findings by Creative Beginnings:
    - Large Gold Lobster Clasp #2624
    - 10 Large Gold Jump Rings #2623
    - 26 Small Gold Jump Rings #2608
    - 2 Gold ½" Necklace Clamps #3815
- 24-gauge gold wire
- Needle nose wire cutter pliers
- Ruler or tape measure

Note:
Adjust length by cutting each strand of thread an extra 1" for each 1" of additional length desired.

Instructions

1: Cut eight strands of solid gold cord each 24" long, cut seven strands of white/gold cord each 24" long.

2: Holding all strands together, tightly wrap the gold wire several times around all strands 2" from one end, covering about ¼". Tie a knot in all strands 6" from wire.

3: For **braiding,** separate the cords as desired into three groups of five cords each. Braid the three groups until you have a braided section 6" long.

4: Tie a knot at the end of the braided section.

5: Tightly wrap the gold wire several times around other ends of the cords 6" from last knot made, covering about ¼". Trim both ends of the necklace to ¼" past the wire.

6: With pliers, fasten a necklace clamp to each end of the necklace, covering the raw ends of the cords. Fasten a jump ring and lobster clasp to one end of the necklace and a jump ring to the opposite end.

7: With pliers, attach a small jump ring to each lightbulb.

8: Using large jump rings to attach each of the large bulbs and small jump rings to attach each of the small bulbs, beginning with a small bulb and alternating large bulbs and small bulbs, attach the jump rings on the lightbulbs to the braided section evenly spaced across *(see photo)*.

Glossary of Wine Terms

Aeration: The process of letting a wine "breathe" in the open air, or swirling wine in a glass. It's debatable whether aerating bottled wines improves their quality. Aeration can soften young, tannic wines; it can fatigue older ones.

Aroma: A term used to describe the smell of wine, specifically it refers to the smells that derive from grapes.

Bite: A marked degree of acidity or tannin. An acid grip in the finish should be more like a zestful tang and is tolerable only in a rich, full-bodied wine.

Body: The weight of wine in your mouth. Alcohol makes a wine seem heavier, as does tannin. Commonly expressed as full-bodied, medium-bodied or medium-weight, or light-bodied.

Bouquet: A tasting term used to describe the smell of the wine as it matures in the bottle. Aroma denotes the smell of the grape.

Brut: French word for 'dry'.

Crisp: A tasting term that denotes a fresh, young wine with good acidity.

Delicate: Used to describe light-to-medium weight wines with good flavors.

Depth: Describes the complexity and concentration of flavors in a wine, as in a wine with excellent or uncommon depth.

Fermentation: Grape sugar is converted into alcohol and carbon dioxide by the action of yeast. For dry wines the process is allowed to continue until all the sugar has been converted into alcohol.

Finish: The taste that remains in the mouth after swallowing. A 'long finish' is desired in a good wine.

Port: A very richly flavored and sweet wine.

Robust: Means full-bodied, intense and vigorous, possibly a bit overblown.

Tannin: A substance found in the skin of grapes that is a necessary component of wine that is to be aged.

Yeast: Promotes fermentation of grape juice. The 'dust' on a grape, known as the 'bloom' is wild yeast.

Towel Rose Gift Box

Designed by Kenna Prior

Finished Size:
Box is 5½" deep x 9¾" square.

Materials:
- 9¾"-square embossed paper maché box
- 3½ yds. fruit-print 2½"-wide wire-edge ribbon
- Americana® Acrylic Paints by DecoArt™:
  Buttermilk #DA3
  Golden Straw #DA168
- Americana® Matte #DAS13 Acrylic Sealer/Finisher by DecoArt™
- 6 cream and 6 sage kitchen towels
- ½" Wash Series 7550 Paintbrush by Loew-Cornell®
- Floral wire
- Disposable paint palette or paper plate
- Ruler
- Pencil
- Wire cutters
- Sewing needle and thread
- Fabri-Tac™ by Beacon™ or fabric glue

Box

1: With the wash brush and buttermilk, paint the outer sides, the bottom and lid of the box; let dry. Apply a second coat of buttermilk and let dry.

2: Paint the inside of the lid and box with buttermilk paint; let dry.

3: Apply a second coat to the inside of the box and lid using golden straw paint; let dry.

4: To highlight the raised areas of the embossing on the lid and box, pour a small amount of golden straw onto the paint palette; dip your fingertip in the paint and dab off some of the excess paint on the palette. Lightly rub your fingertip over the embossed areas of the box; let dry.

5: To draw the plaid pattern on the bottom of the box *(see plaid pattern on lid in photo)*, making very faint marks with the pencil, evenly space 11 lines across the bottom of the box. Working horizontally across the first lines, evenly space 11 more lines across the bottom of the box to complete the plaid.

6: To draw the stripes on the sides of the box, continue the lines from the plaid pattern on the bottom across each side, skipping over the embossed area.

7: Place the lid on the box; skipping over the embossed area, continue drawing lines across the lid to match the stripes on the sides of the box.

8: On the bottom of the box, using the wash brush and golden straw, paint over each line in one direction, then paint over

Continued on page 106

Victorian Christmas Basket

**Designed by
Deborah Levy-Hamburg**

Finished Size:
About 17" including trim.

Materials:
- Large gold-painted wicker basket
- Gold crochet doily to cover the top of the basket
- Assorted memorabilia — doll, framed photo, Christmas card, Christmas ornament, small figurines, jewelry pieces *(old or new)*, etc.
- Small bag of Christmas potpourri
- Large white flower with gold trim
- 72" strand of gold/copper beaded garland
- 4 large sheets of craft paper or wrapping paper
- Sheet of gold tissue paper
- 12"-long wooden skewer
- 2"-wide transparent tape
- 20-gauge gold wire
- 14"-long bundle of gold-painted grapevine branches
- Wire cutters
- Crafty® Magic Melt® Oval Magic Pro Glue Gun by Adhesive Technologies, Inc.
- Crafty® Magic Melt® Glue Sticks by Adhesive Technologies, Inc.

Instructions

1: With your hands, lightly crumple each of the sheets of craft paper into a medium size ball; place the paper balls in the bottom of the basket.

2: Fold the sheet of gold tissue paper in half; lay the paper over the top of the basket and tuck in the edges to cover the craft paper.

3: For the grapevine trim, cut two 10" pieces of wire; gather the center of the grapevine branches and wrap them with one piece of wire to secure. Tuck the bottom two or three inches of the branches down into the basket next to the handle. Attach the branches to the handle of the basket with the other 10" piece of wire; cut off any excess wire.

4: Place the gold doily over the top of the basket covering the gold tissue paper and hiding the ends of the grapevine branches; allow the doily to drape over the front edge of the basket.

5: Measure the height of the Christmas card and add 4". With the wire cutters, removing excess length from the flat end of the skewer, cut the skewer to that length. Tape the skewer to the center back of the Christmas card with the

Continued on page 106

Victorian Christmas Basket
Continued from page 105

flat edge of the skewer down about ½" from the top of the card.

6: With the back of the basket facing you and the card facing toward the front of the basket, holding the pointed end of the skewer about 2" from the back edge of the basket, poke the skewer through the doily and down through the papers as far as it will go.

7: With the front of the basket facing you, place the doll in a sitting position toward the right side of the basket, leaning her against the card and against the handle of the basket. If desired, the doll can be secured with glue or she can be wired to the handle of the basket.

8: Glue one end of the beaded garland to the inside rim of the basket next to one handle. Wrap the garland around the handle two or three times and across to the other side of the basket, drape the garland back and forth across the front of the basket *(see photo)*, gluing in place as needed; wind any remaining garland around on top of the gold doily.

9: Place the framed photo on the left side of the basket leaning against the handle; wire or glue the frame to the basket handle to secure.

10: Place the Christmas ornament in the center front of the basket and glue or wire in place.

11: To fill in the area behind the framed photo, lay the flower in the basket, slightly tilted toward the front; glue in place.

12: Decorate or fill in any remaining areas with small figurines, jewelry, ornaments or other memorabilia as desired *(see photo)*; glue in place if needed.

13: Sprinkle a small amount of potpourri around the basket.

Towel Rose Gift Box
Continued from page 102

each line in the other direction; let dry.

9: In the same manner, paint the plaid pattern on the lid; let dry.

10: Paint the stripes on the sides of the box; let dry.

11: Apply a coat of spray sealer to all surfaces of the box and lid; let dry. Apply a second coat of sealer and let dry.

12: Cut two pieces of ribbon each 22" long. Fold the end of one ribbon under ½"; glue the fold even with the top edge and centered on one side of the box *(see photo)*. Wrap the ribbon around the bottom and up the other side to the edge of the box; fold the end under ½" and glue in place. Repeat with the remaining 22" piece of ribbon on the other sides of the box.

13: Cut two pieces of ribbon each 15" long. Matching the placement of the ribbon on the box, wrap the ribbons across the lid with 1" on each end of the ribbon being tucked to the inside of the lid; glue ends in place.

14: Fold the remaining ribbon into a 9"-wide, four-loop bow and wrap the center of the bow with a 3" piece of floral wire; twist to secure. Glue the bow to the center of the lid.

Towel Rose

1: For the **leaves**, fold one sage towel in half lengthwise; with needle and a double strand of thread, run a gathering thread through both layers of the towel about ¼" from the fold. Pull the thread to gather very tightly and secure the thread.

2: In the same manner, run another gathering thread from the center of the fold down to the bottom edge of the towel. Pull the thread to gather very tightly and secure the thread.

3: For the **rose**, place one cream-colored towel flat on the work surface; fold each short end of the towel so the edges meet at the center *(see step 1 of Folding illustration)*.

4: Carefully turn the towel over; fold in half again, bringing the bottom fold up to meet the top fold *(see step 2 of Folding illustration)*.

5: With the two folds at the top and the center fold and two hemmed edges at the bottom, fold the upper corners of the towel down to meet the bottom fold *(see step 3 of Folding illustration)*.

6: With the needle and a double strand of thread, working through all thicknesses of the towel, run a gathering thread across the bottom edge of the towel *(see dotted line in step 3 of Folding illustration)*. Pull the thread to gather; while gathering, roll the gathered edge to form the rose. When satisfied with the shape of the rose, pull the thread to gather tightly and secure.

7: Wrap the center of an 18" piece of floral wire tightly around the base of the rose. Spread the wire ends apart and wrap them tightly around the center of the leaves.

8: Neatly fold the remaining towels and place them in the box as a gift.

9: Place the rose and leaves in the box or display on top of the box beside the bow.

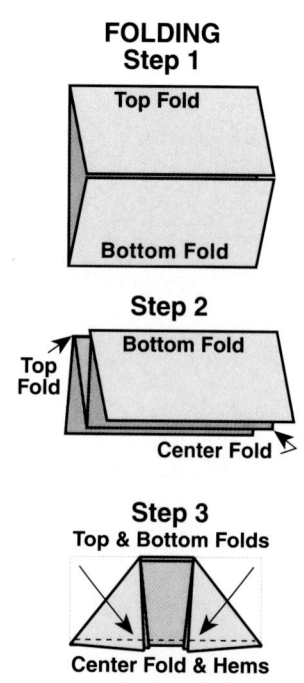

FOLDING
Step 1 — Top Fold / Bottom Fold
Step 2 — Top Fold / Bottom Fold / Center Fold
Step 3 — Top & Bottom Folds / Center Fold & Hems

Santa's Magic Key

Designed by Florence Tebbets

Materials:
- Spare household or auto key with large grip
- 3" x 5" unruled index card or cardstock
- Americana® Acrylic Paints by DecoArt®:
    - Medium Flesh #DA102
    - Lamp Black #DA67
    - Titanium White #DA1
- Christmas Red #DCA20 Crafter's Acrylics by DecoArt™
- Snow-Tex™ by DecoArt™ *(snow paint)*
- Americana® Matte Sealer/Finisher #DAS137 by DecoArt™
- Craft Picks by Forster® or toothpicks
- #4 or #6 flat paintbrush
- Iridescent glitter
- 12" piece of gold cord
- Black fine-tip permanent marker
- Disposable paint palette or paper plate
- Small amount of vinegar
- Hole punch
- Scrap piece of Styrofoam®
- Decorative-edge scissors
- Spray glitter *(optional)*

Instructions
1. Thoroughly wash and dry the key with soap and water. To remove all traces of oil and dirt, rinse the key in a solution of half water, half vinegar; dry completely.
2. Insert the bottom of the key into the center of the scrap of Styrofoam 1"; then remove the key and set Styrofoam aside. This will be used later to store the key while it dries.
3. Using the photo as a guide for all painting, for **Santa's face,** with medium flesh, paint a small circle on the center front of the key grip; let dry. Apply a second coat if needed for total coverage.
4. For the **hat,** with Christmas red, paint the upper half of the key grip on both sides; let dry. Apply a second coat if needed.
5. For the **eyes,** dip the small tip of a craft pick in the lamp black and dot two eyes centered on the face area of the key; let dry. In the same manner, highlight the eyes by placing a small dot of white in the center of each eye.
6. For the **nose,** with the marker, draw an inverted U.
7. For the **hair and beard,** use the thicker end of a craft pick to apply the snow paint in a dabbing motion around the sides of the face, under the chin and below the hat on the back of the key grip. In the same manner, apply a ring of snow paint around the base of the hat to form a "fur" brim and apply a small mound of snow paint to the top of the keyhole for the pom-pom.
8. Place a small amount of snow paint on the palette and stir in a little of the iridescent glitter. Using a pick, apply this glitter paint on top of the fur brim and the pom-pom. Place the key upright in the styrofoam and allow the snow paint to dry 2–6 hours until hard.
9. Spray both sides of the key with sealer/finisher; let dry.
10. Using the decorative scissors, cut the cardstock into a 2½" x 4½" oval *(or desired shape)*. Punch a hole in the top of the card.
11. On the card, using the marker, write desired message or the message shown in the photo: "Dear Santa, We don't have a fireplace so please use this 'Magic Key' to unlock the front door. Thank You." Have your child or children sign the card.
12. Fold the gold cord in half and insert the folded end through the key hole, insert the ends of the cord through the fold and pull tight. Tie the card to the ends of the cord. If desired, spray the card and key with the spray glitter; let dry. Hang the card on the front door on Christmas Eve.

Holiday Bird Feeder and Birdhouse

Designed by Marilyn Shelton

Finished Sizes:
Bird Feeder is about 10" tall without hanger.
Birdhouse is about 15½" tall.

Materials:
- Walnut #D529 Gel Stain™ by DecoArt™
- Americana® Acrylic Paints by DecoArt™:
    Hauser Dark Green #DA133
    Cranberry Wine #DA112
    Titanium (Snow) White #DA01
- Glorious Gold #DA71 Dazzling Metallics™ Acrylic Paint by DecoArt™
- Americana® Matte Acrylic Sealer/Finisher #DAS13 by DecoArt™
- Outdoor Snow #DAR169 Patio Paint™ by DecoArt™
- ½"-wide flat paintbrush
- Craft sticks
- ½"-wide painter's tape or masking tape
- Crafty® Magic Melt® Oval Magic Pro Glue Gun by Adhesive Technologies, Inc.
- Crafty® Magic Melt® Glue Sticks by Adhesive Technologies, Inc.

Additional Materials for Bird Feeder:
- 8½" Natural Wood Octagon Bird Feeder #9157-38 by By Darice®
- Decorations by Jazz Ups™:
    2 Wreaths #4481
    2 Snowmen #4516
    2 Christmas Trees #4486
    2 Candy Canes #4504
- Small pinecone
- 2" piece of 18-gauge wire
- ¼ cup creamy peanut butter
- Wild bird birdseed
- Needle nose pliers

Additional Materials for Birdhouse:
- 15½" Wood Birdhouse With 3 Holes #CPW9928 by Wangs International, Inc.
- Decorations by Jazz Ups™:
    1 Wreath #4529
    1 Poinsettia #4474
    1 Small Holly Leaf #4478
    2 Large Holly Leaves #4477
    1 Candy Cane #4504
- Timeless Minis™ "Let It Snow" Sign #2306-50 by Darice®
- Ruler
- Pencil

Note:
To tape off an area that is not being painted or stained, cut a piece of masking tape or painter's tape to fit and apply it to that area. Firmly press the tape in place so paint or stain will not seep under it.

Bird Feeder
1: Lift the roof off of the feeder, sliding it down the length of the rope and set it aside; carefully remove the glass sides from the feeder. Use the painter's tape or masking tape (see Note) to tape off the green slatted outer edge and eaves of the roof (see photo), leaving the bottom of the roof exposed for staining. In the same manner, tape off the cranberry base of the feeder, leaving the sides and inner bottom piece exposed for staining. Tape off the portion of the rope that is inside the feeder to protect it from being stained.

2: Following the manufacturer's instructions, using the paintbrush, apply the gel stain to the bottom of the roof, the sides and the inner bottom piece of the feeder; let dry. Remove the tape.

Continued on page 113

Sweet Indulgence

Designed by Kenna Prior

Finished Size:
Box is 8" x 11" x 4¼" deep, plus contents.

Materials:
- 8" x 11" x 4¼" deep Oval Shaker Box by Darice®
- Americana® Acrylic Paints by DecoArt™:
    - Buttermilk #DA3
    - Soft Peach #DA216
    - Antique Green #DA147
    - Celery Green #DA208
    - Camel #DA191
    - Antique Mauve #DA162
    - Sable Brown #DA61
    - Desert Sand #DA77
    - Heritage Black #DA219
- Americana® Matte Finish #DAS13 Sealer/Finisher by DecoArt™
- Paintbrushes by Loew-Cornell®:
    - ½" Wash Series 7550
    - #2 Liner Series 7050
    - #6 Round Series 7000
    - ¼" Stippler Series 7850
    - ¼" Angular Shader Series 7400
- Natural color excelsior
- Small book ("The Art of Doing Nothing" by Vienne & Lennard is shown in photo)
- Bookmark
- Small bottle of Bailey's Irish Creme liquor or desired beverage
- 2 chocolate candy bars
- 2 stems of silk flower buds with leaves
- Small paper napkin (any kind)
- Disposable paint palette or paper plate
- Pencil
- Ruler
- Ingredients for candy recipes or purchased candies
- Gold foil candy cups (optional)
- Transparent tape (optional)
- Several strands of raffia (optional)
- Cellophane or plastic wrap (optional)

Painting

1: Remove the lid from the box and set aside. Open up the paper napkin and drape it across the front edge of the box, half in and half out (see the painted napkin on box in photo). With the pencil, lightly draw the outline of the napkin on the inside and outside of the box.

2: With the ½" wash brush and buttermilk, paint the solid portion of the napkin. Let dry.

Continued on page 112

Sweet Indulgence
Continued from page 111

3: The **lace trim** on the napkin can be painted freehand or the pencil can be used to lightly draw the lace trim as desired before painting. Using the liner brush and buttermilk, paint the lace trim around the entire napkin; let dry.

4: For the **string of pearls,** to mark the center of each pearl across the inside and outside of the box, with the pencil, draw a curved row of dots spaced about 3/8" apart *(see photo)*. Using the 1/4" shader brush and soft peach, paint a C stroke *(see illustration)* on the left side of each pencil dot and a C stroke in the opposite direction on the right side of each dot to form pearls; let dry.

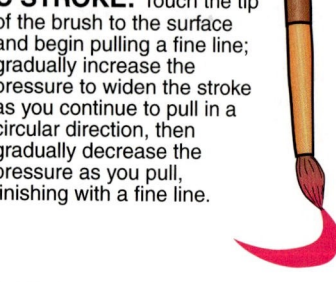

C STROKE: Touch the tip of the brush to the surface and begin pulling a fine line; gradually increase the pressure to widen the stroke as you continue to pull in a circular direction, then gradually decrease the pressure as you pull, finishing with a fine line.

5: For the **highlights** on each pearl, with the same brush and buttermilk, paint a smaller C stroke on the left side of each pearl; let dry.

6: For the **painted raffia tie** around the box, place the lid on the box; with the pencil, lightly draw a line around the entire box in both directions with the ties crossing on the left side of the lid *(see photo)*. Lightly draw a single bow loop and one streamer in the upper left portion of the lid for a partial bow. Remove the lid.

7: With the liner brush and antique green thinned with a small amount of water, paint the bow loop, the ties and the streamer lines on the lid and the box, keeping in mind that this is a natural fiber tie and the lines do not have to be perfect. Let dry. With the same brush and thinned celery green, paint long, thin lines on top of the ties and bow loop for highlights; let dry.

8: For the **lilac spray,** using the stipple brush and heritage black, paint a base coat in the shape of a lilac spray on the lid *(see photo)*; let dry.

9: Using the shader brush and antique mauve, paint 1/2"-wide four-petaled Flowers *(see illustration)* randomly across the basecoat of the lilac spray, extending some flowers slightly beyond the edge of the basecoat; let dry.

FLOWER

10: In the same manner, double load *(see illustration)* the shader brush with antique mauve and buttermilk and randomly paint flowers over the same area allowing some of the first layer of flowers to show through; let dry.

DOUBLE LOAD

11: For the **stem and leaves,** double load the liner brush with thinned antique green and thinned buttermilk; with the green side against the lid, paint long, flowing strokes for the stem and leaves *(see photo)*; let dry.

12: For the **center of each flower,** using the round brush and camel, make a small paint dot in the center of each flower; let dry.

13: For the **tag,** use the pencil to lightly draw the outline of a 1 1/2" x 2 1/2" tag *(see photo)*. With the round brush and desert sand, fill in the tag. While the paint is still wet, add buttermilk to the same brush and working from the center of the tag outward, lightly stroke the buttermilk across the tag.

14: With the liner brush and thinned sable brown, paint "Sweet Indulgence" on the tag and paint a small dot for string hole *(see photo);* let dry.

15: With the liner brush and thinned antique green, paint the string *(see photo)*; let dry.

16: For the **shading,** using the liner brush and thinned sable brown, painting thin lines of shadow at the bottom and to the right of all objects, shade the flower spray, ties, bow, tag, stem and leaves; let dry.

17: In the same manner, with the shader brush and thinned sable brown, paint shading around the lace of the napkin and the pearls that are draped across the brown part of the box. With the same brush and desert sand, shade the pearls that lay across the napkin. Let dry.

18: Spray all surfaces with a coat of sealer; let dry. Repeat two or three times.

Assembly

1: Before adding any of the contents, decide if you will place the lid back on the box for giving or if you would prefer to place the lid underneath the box and display the contents. If you intend to place the lid on the box, fill the box half full with excelsior and wedge the items down into the excelsior as they are added, keeping them below the rim. If you prefer to display the contents, fill the box completely with excelsior and prop the items on top.

2: Place the book, with the bookmark inside, in the back of the box with the bottle of desired beverage laying at an angle in front of the book. Place the two large candy bars at an angle on the right side of the box. Fill in any open areas with the individual candies *(homemade from recipes included or purchased candy)*.

3: Wedging the stems of the flowers and leaves down into the excelsior, place flowers across the front of the box and the leaves toward the back.

4: Wrapping the box and contents with cellophane or plastic wrap is optional. If the box will be presented with the lid on, place a 20" x 22" piece of cellophane or plastic wrap over the top of the assembled contents; using a ruler or similar object, tuck the sides of the wrap down into the box between the box and the excelsior.

5: If the box is to be presented with the lid placed on the bottom of the box and the contents displayed, lay the box centered crosswise on top of a 20" x 50" piece of cellophane or plastic wrap. Pull the long front and back pieces of wrap up evenly over the top of the box, gather the wrap accordion style with your hands about five inches above the contents, tie the raffia strands around the gathers to secure. Trim the raffia strands to the desired length.

6: Fold the open sides of the wrap into neat pleats and secure with tape.

Raspberry Curd Truffles
1/4 cup Dickinson's Raspberry Curd

¼ cup half and half cream
25 pieces Wilton White Candy Melts
1 pkg. Wilton Dark Cocoa Candy Melts
Red food coloring
Wax paper-lined cookie sheet
Aluminum foil
Toothpicks
2 sandwich-size plastic bags

Bring cream to a light boil over medium heat. Add curd and 20 white candy melts; stirring continuously, return to a boil and remove from heat. Continue stirring until mixture is smooth and satiny. Cover and refrigerate for 30 minutes or until firm. Quickly roll mixture into ½" to 1" balls; place on wax paper-lined cookie sheet and return to refrigerator. Place cocoa candy melts into a small plastic bowl and microwave on high, stirring every 45 to 60 seconds, until melted. Dip white candy balls into the melted cocoa candy and place them on a sheet of foil until set. Dip each candy a second time, reheating cocoa candy as needed.

Place five remaining white candy melts into a plastic bag and microwave until melted. Stir in a drop of red food coloring and mix thoroughly. Cut a tiny point from one corner of the bag and drizzle the melted candy across the candy balls as desired. Place candies in gold foil cups.

Painted Candies
20–40 Wilton Dark Cocoa Candy Melts
20 Wilton White Candy Melts
Wilton Roses Candy Mold
2 small freezer strength plastic kitchen bags
Wilton Candy Painting Palette Set

Place two of the dark candy melts on the candy palette and microwave on high, stirring at 30 second intervals until melted. Using the paintbrush, paint the roses and stems in the bottom of each candy mold; refrigerate until set. Place 20 white candy melts in a plastic bag and microwave until melted. Cut a tiny point from one corner of the bag with scissors. Using the bag as a piping bag, squeeze a thin layer of white candy over the painted roses. Refrigerate until set. Repeat this process with the remaining cocoa candy melts. When the candy is completely set, remove them from the mold and place in gold foil cups.

Holiday Bird Feeder and Birdhouse
Continued from page 108

3: Tape off the stained areas under the eaves of the roof, on the sides and the bottom of the feeder; tape off the bottom ring of the knob on the rooftop.
4: With the paintbrush and hauser green, paint the eaves and the slatted top of the roof *(see photo)*; let dry.
5: With cranberry, paint the base of the feeder and the bottom ring of the knob on the roof; let dry. Remove the tape.
6: With the gold paint, paint the top portion of the knob on the roof; let dry.
7: Following the manufacturer's instructions, apply a coat of sealer to each painted and stained surface of the feeder; let dry.
8: Reassemble the feeder. With hot glue, attach one wreath to one stained side of the roof, attach the remaining wreath to the opposite side of the roof. Glue each candy cane, snowman and tree around the base of the feeder *(see photo)*.
9: Following the manufacturer's instructions, using the craft sticks, apply snow around the rooftop and base of the feeder as shown in the photo; let dry.
10: Reserving ¼ cup of seed for the pinecone, fill the feeder with birdseed and hang outside.
11: For the **peanut butter pinecone**, glue one end of the 2" wire to the bottom of the pinecone; bend the opposite end into a hook with the pliers. Mix ¼ cup peanut butter with ¼ cup of the birdseed; stir together well. With a craft stick, spread the mixture over the pinecone, pushing it into the crevices. Hang the pinecone from the bottom of the Feeder.

Birdhouse
1: Using the masking tape or painter's tape, tape off the top and bottom of the roof *(see Note)*; tape off ½" on the edge of each side of each corner of the house to be painted with white and cranberry checks later *(see photo)*.
2: Following the manufacturer's instructions, using the paintbrush, apply the gel stain to the sides of the house; let dry. Remove the tape.
3: Tape off the stained house sides, the unstained house corners, the cranberry-colored beam across the top of the roof and the gingerbread trim at the peak of the roof *(see photo)*.
4: With the paintbrush and hauser green, paint the top and bottom of the roof; let dry. Remove the tape.
5: With cranberry, paint the gingerbread trim, the beam on the roof and the bottom portion of the two knobs on top of the roof; let dry.
6: With gold, paint the top portion of the knobs on the roof; let dry. With green, paint the rings around the bottom of the knobs *(see photo)*; let dry.
7: For the squares in the unstained area along the sides of the house, with the ruler and pencil, starting at the bottom of the house, draw a line every ¾" up the side. Paint all of the white squares *(see photo)*; let dry. Paint all of the cranberry squares; let dry.
8: Following the manufacturer's instructions, apply a coat of sealer to each painted and stained surface of the birdhouse; let dry.
9: With hot glue, attach the candy cane to the gingerbread trim, the wreath above the top hole, the poinsettia above the middle hole, the small holly leaves above the bottom hole and the two large holly leaves to each side of the house.
10: Following the manufacturer's instructions, using the craft sticks, apply snow on the rooftop, around each hole and across the top of the "Let It Snow" sign (see photo); let dry.
11: Hang the sign on the bottom perch, secure with glue if desired.

Christmas Potpourri Pillow

Designed by Michele Wilcox

Finished Size:
6½" x 10½".

Materials:
- 2 pieces of desired fabric each 7" x 11" — shown in photo is gold satin brocade fabric
- Polyester fiberfill
- Small amount of potpourri
- 3" Christmas floral pick
- 36" of 2½"-wide wire-edge Christmas ribbon
- Sewing needle and thread

Instructions
1: Place the fabric pieces right sides together. Allowing ¼" for the seams, sew across both long sides and one short side, leaving one short side open for stuffing. Turn the fabric right side out.
2: Firmly stuff three-fourths of the pillow with fiberfill. Hollow out the center of the fiberfill and fill with a small amount of potpourri; finish stuffing the pillow with fiberfill.
3: Tucking the seam allowance in as you go, sew the remaining side closed.
4: Wrap the ribbon around the center of the pillow and tie it in a 5"-wide, single-loop bow; trim the ribbon ends in a V *(see photo)*.
5: Trim the wire end of the Christmas pick and insert the wire into the bow. If desired, the pick may be sewn or glued in place on the pillow.

❋ Potpourri Making

With the amazing selection of fresh and dried flowers available these days, there is no reason why every room in our homes cannot be enriched with the delights of potpourri.

1: Start with the dried materials. Choose the best quality blooms and leaves you can find, or grow your own and completely dry them.

2: Place dried materials in a glass or glazed pottery bowl to mix. Using two new wooden spoons, toss lightly.

3: Sprinkle on the dried herbs, berries, seeds and/or spices. Again, toss lightly.

4: In a separate bowl mix together measured amounts of fixative and essential oils. Adjust amount of scent to suit yourself.

Orris root, from the florentine iris, is a readily available and popular fixative. It "takes" the scent of the oils applied to it. Oak moss, vetiver and benzoin are also good fixatives.

Using eyedroppers or dispensing bottles, drop essential oils onto fixative and mix. Then combine gently with rest of potpourri.

Age potpourri in a roomy, but tightly closed paper bag lined with waxed paper in a cool, dark place. Stir mixture every few days, and allow to cure for three to six weeks before use.

Refresh potpourri by sprinkling with a few drops of essential oils and tossing gently to mix.

Happy Holidays

2 cups red and green eucalyptus sprigs
1 cup oak moss
White sorghum tips
Generous sprigs of nandina or holly berry or bittersweet
Pine branch tips
Small golden ball ornaments
Star anise (optional)
7 drops bayberry oil
3 drops myrrh oil
1-2 drops eucalyptus oil (optional)

Drop essential oils onto bits of oak moss and blend. Optional additions are miniature pinecones, cinnamon sticks and frankincense tears.

Candles

Designed by Marilyn Shelton

Angel Candle

Finished Size:
Candle is 6" high and 6" in diameter.

Materials:
- 6"-diameter vanilla or desired-scent candle
- Gold Angels by Jazz Ups™:
    - 4 Sitting Angels #1994
    - 4 Kneeling Angels (left) #1991L
    - 4 Kneeling Angels (right) #1991R
    - 4 Tumbling Angels (left) #1972L
    - 4 Tumbling Angels (right) #1972R
    - 4 Flying Angels (left) #1909L
    - 4 Flying Angels (right) #1909R
- Crafty® Magic Melt® Floral Pro™ Glue Gun by Adhesive Technologies, Inc.
- Crafty® Magic Melt® Floral Glue Sticks by Adhesive Technologies, Inc.

Instructions

1. Glue the four sitting angels evenly spaced around the bottom edge of the candle as shown in the photo.
2. Glue a left kneeling angel and a right kneeling angel beside each sitting angel *(facing the sitting angel — see photo)*.
3. Working around the candle, glue the four left flying angels in a group on one side *(see photo)* and the four right flying angels in a group on the opposite side.
4. Working between the groups of flying angels, glue the left tumbling angels in a circle on one side of the candle and glue the right tumbling angels in a circle on the opposite side of the candle.

Ivory Christmas Candle

Finished Size:
Candle is 4" high and 3" in diameter.

Materials:
- 3"-diameter vanilla or desired-scent candle
- Christmas Ornaments by Jazz Ups™:
    - Sleigh #4390
    - Santa Claus #4387
    - 6 Reindeer #4388
    - Snowman #4405
    - 2 Candy Canes #4412
    - Angel on Moon #4429
    - Christmas Tree With Snow #4396
- Crafty® Magic Melt® Floral Pro™ Glue Gun by Adhesive Technologies, Inc.
- Crafty® Magic Melt® Floral Glue Sticks by Adhesive Technologies, Inc.

Instructions

1. Glue each of the Christmas ornaments to the candle, with the sleigh at the bottom edge of the candle and the Santa standing just to the right of the sleigh.
2. Glue three pairs of reindeer in front of the sleigh as if they are flying across the sky pulling the sleigh.
3. On the side of the candle opposite the sleigh, glue the Christmas tree with snowman standing beside it; glue a candy cane on either side of the tree and snowman.
4. In the remaining open area at the top of the candle, glue the moon with the angel.

Twelve Days of Christmas Candle

Select a special Christmas scented candle to be delivered on the Twelfth Day before Christmas. Paint the numbers counting off to Christmas Day ("12, 11, 10, 9, 8, 7, 6, 5, 4, 3, 2, 1") at equal intervals down the side of the candle, using paint with a candle wax medium added. Insert the candle in a small candleholder wrapped in a cheerful Christmas ribbon and present to special friends or family with this holiday note:

Place this little candle
Where your family gathers 'round
And count the days 'til Christmas
As you watch it burning down.
Light your Christmas candle
On the thirteenth of December,
Then burn each day that follows,
Don't forget now to remember!
By the time you reach the candle's end,
It will be Christmas Day
But you'll never reach the end
Of the love we send your way!

Merry Christmas
Sign with your family name

CHAPTER FOUR
Holiday Home

Brimming with gaiety and cheer, an open house is the perfect setting for sharing the joys of the season with friends and family. Being the perfect holiday hostess has never been easier.

Embossed Felt
Mantle Scarf

Designed by Blanche Lind

Finished Size:
16" wide x 70" long without trim.

Materials:
- 16" x 70" piece of Hunter Green #472 Tooled Leather Classic Impressions™ Embossed Felt by Kunin Felt
- ½ yd. of metallic gold woven fabric
- 12 skeins of Gold #5282 Six-Strand Metallic Embroidery Floss Art. 317 by DMC®
- 70" of yellow ½"-wide satin ribbon
- Liqui-Fuse™ Liquid Fusible Web by Beacon™
- Fray Check™ by Dritz
- Iron
- Pressing cloth
- Spray bottle of water
- Tape measure or ruler
- Disappearing ink marker or chalk pencil

Tassels

1: From two skeins of embroidery floss, cut ten 36"-long pieces and ten 7"-long pieces.

2: For each **tassel** *(make 10)*, tie one 7"-long piece of floss around the center of one full skein of floss *(see A on illustration)* and fold the skein in half; about 1" from the fold, wrap one 36"-long piece several times around all the strands and tie the ends in a knot *(see B on illustration)*. Remove the labels, cut the loops at ends of all strands and trim the ends even.

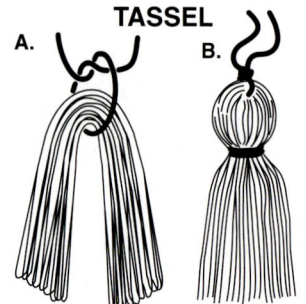

Mantle Scarf

1: Cut nine 4" x 7" rectangles from the gold fabric. To keep the fabric of each rectangle from fraying, run a bead of fray check along each edge; let dry.

2: For each **gold point** *(make 9)*, with the right side of one gold rectangle facedown, fold the upper corner on each 4" side down and into the center, forming a triangle *(see Gold Triangle illustration)*; with the iron and a damp pressing cloth, press each fold flat.

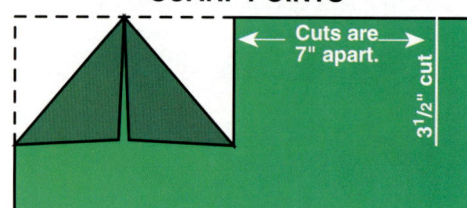

3: Following the manufacturer's instructions, apply liquid fusible web on the inside of each gold point; press with the iron and damp pressing cloth to fuse.

4: For the **mantle scarf,** use the ruler to measure every 7" along one 70" side of the felt, then use the marker or pencil to draw a 3½"-long line in from the edge at each mark; cut along each line *(see Scarf Points illustration)*.

5: For each **point on the scarf**, with the right side of the fabric facedown, fold both corners of each 7" section down to the center; with the iron and damp pressing cloth, press each fold flat.

6: In the same manner as the gold points, apply liquid fusible web to the inside of each point on the mantle scarf and insert the tie ends of one tassel, allowing the tassel to hang from the point *(see photo)* and press as before to fuse.

7: Apply a bead of liquid fusible web along the front straight edge of one gold point; place the point facedown centered in the opening between two points on the felt, matching all points; repeat with the remaining gold points.

8: Apply a bead of liquid fusible web along the long straight edges of all the gold points; lay the ribbon over the bead of liquid fusible web and, with the iron and the pressing cloth, fuse the gold points to the felt and the ribbon.

Victorian Christmas Boxes

Designed by Rona Riley

Finished Sizes:
Large box is 15½" wide x 16" high x 9" deep; Small box is 13½" wide x 14" high x 6½" deep.

Materials:
- 16" paper maché Christmas tree-shaped box with lid
- 14" paper maché Christmas tree-shaped box with lid
- Rose #2415 Spray Paint by Krylon®
- ½ yd. of muslin
- ½ yd. of 1"-thick polyester foam quilt batting
- 6" x 54" piece of burgundy moiré taffeta fabric
- 8" x 54" mauve moiré taffeta fabric
- Several ¼ yd. pieces of desired coordinating fabrics for quilted top — shown in photo are:
    - Brocades
    - Satins
    - Velvets
    - Taffetas
    - Floral-print cottons
- Sulky® Rayon 30-weight Embroidery Thread:
    - Spool of Pink #1121
    - Spool of Burgundy #1034
    - Spool of True Green #1101
    - Spool of White #1001
- Spool of Gold #7007 Sulky® Original Metallic Rayon 30-weight Embroidery Thread
- Brass Charms by Creative Beginnings:
    - Heart with Keyhole #6096
    - Cupid FR #6204
    - Fan #1271
    - Double Cupid #1814
    - Rose Branch #1872
    - Floral Scroll #1224
- Assorted sizes and colors of Ribbon Roses by Offray
- Assorted sizes and colors of Flat Back Crystals and Pearls by National Art Craft
- 2 yds. of 4 mm iridescent strung pearls
- 2 white 3"-wide crochet doilies
- Assorted lace appliqués by Wrights®
- Several different 2 yd. pieces of ⅜"-wide to ⅝"-wide assorted plain or metallic braids and/or trims by Wrights *(for trim around box lid; ends may be used for trimming on quilted top)*
- Memory Craft® 9000 Sewing Machine by Janome Sewing Machine Co. or sewing machine with

Continued on page 129

Holiday Home ~ page 123

Glass Ornament Wreath

Designed by Marilyn Shelton

Finished Size:
29" across.

Materials:
- 24" Styrofoam® wreath by Floracraft
- Glass Christmas Ornaments by Rauch™ Industries:
    2⅝"-across *(large)*:
    12 Purple #8168-286
    12 Bright Green #8168-05
    12 Turquoise Candy #6002-92
    12 Opalescent #8168-57 *(white)*
    12 Burgundy #8168-325
    12 Royal Blue #8168-18
    12 Red #8168-09
    2"-across *(medium)*:
    10 Silver #8012-07
    10 Royal Blue #8012-04
    1¾"-across *(small)*:
    18 Silver #8015-07
    18 Burgundy #8015-02
- 150 bamboo skewers each 12"-long — one for each ornament, plus a few extra
- Spool of 3"-wide Silver Firefly Wire Edge Ribbon by Offray
- 18" of 18-gauge floral stem wire
- Silver QuickSnip™ Foil Wire by FibreCraft®
- Wire cutting pliers
- EZ Bowmaker *(optional)*
- Craft & Floral Pro™ Glue Gun by Adhesive Technologies, Inc.
- Crafty® Magic Melt® Floral Glue Sticks by Adhesive Technologies, Inc.

Instructions

1: For the **hanger,** wrap the floral stem wire around the Styrofoam wreath; with the pliers, twist the ends of the wire together to secure.

2: For **each ornament,** remove the metal top and the wire hanger from each ornament; glue the metal top to the ornament. Place a drop of glue on the flat end of one bamboo skewer; insert the skewer through the opening in the metal top and glue to the bottom of the ornament.

3: With an unused bamboo skewer, punch a starter hole in the foam wreath where you wish to place an ornament. Beginning with the larger of the glass ornaments and

Continued on page 128

Santa Claus

Designed by Jean Ashley

Finished Size:
About 18" tall.

Materials:
- 3¾" porcelain Santa head and hands
- ½ yd. of burgundy/taupe gingham check fabric
- ½ yd. of burgundy cotton velvet fabric
- ¼ yd. of 36"-wide light brown fake fur
- 8" x 10" sheet of brown felt
- Quilt batting
- 15" high clear acrylic cone
- 3 yds. of 1¼"-wide burgundy/metallic gold braided trim
- ½ yd. of ⅝"-wide burgundy velvet ribbon
- 8" of craft wire
- 4½"-high sisal Christmas tree with snow
- 12 gold 6 mm beads
- Miniature teddy bear
- Miniature violin
- 2 miniature gift packages
- Sewing needle and burgundy thread
- Tape measure
- Crafty® Magic Melt® Oval Magic Pro Glue Gun by Adhesive Technologies, Inc.
- Crafty® Magic Melt® Glue Sticks by Adhesive Technologies, Inc.

Instructions

1: For the **arms**, cut a 7" x 18" piece of gingham fabric and a 7" x 18" piece of quilt batting. Lay the fabric facedown with the quilt batting on top; fold one long edge of both fabric and batting into center about 3" and glue in several places to hold. Along the opposite side, fold ½" of fabric over the batting and glue to hold; matching the first fold, overlap the fabric and batting, forming a tube and glue the edges together along the entire length.

2: For **each hand,** at one end of the arms, insert one hand; gather the fabric around the hand and glue the gathers to the hand. Cut a piece of velvet ribbon to fit around the gathers and glue in place for a cuff.

3: From the quilt batting cut a 7" x 13" piece.

4: For the **body,** spread glue on the upper 7" of the acrylic cone; press one 7" edge of the batting vertically on the glue and wrap the batting around the cone, gluing the other edge in place beside the first edge.

5: On the right side of the fabric, run a bead of glue along one long edge of the remaining gingham fabric; fold in half right sides together, matching edges to form a tube.

6: For the **robe,** place the fabric tube over the body. Matching the top of the body with the top edge of the tube, fold and pleat to gather the fabric to fit around the top of the cone. Wrap the 8" of craft wire around the fabric gathers about ½" from the top of the cone; tightly

Continued on page 128

Santa Claus
Continued from page 126

twist the wire ends together to secure. Loosely pleat the fabric around the cone and glue the bottom edge of the robe to the inside at the bottom of the cone.

7: With the seam of the robe at the back, glue the Santa head in place on the top of the body.
8: Spread glue on about 4" at the center of the arms; just below the bottom edge of the back of the head, with the left hand on the left side of the body and the right hand on the right side of the body, press the center of the arms to the body.
9: For the **hood,** cut a 4" x 7" piece of burgundy velvet; run a bead of glue along one 7" side. Folding the piece in half with right sides together, match the edges and press to adhere.
10: For the **cape,** cut a 16" x 36" piece of burgundy velvet; run a gathering thread along one 36" side. Pull the thread to tightly gather the fabric to 7" wide and secure the thread. With right sides together, match the gathered edge with the bottom of the hood; allow ½" for a seam and sew the pieces together.
11: For **fur trim,** measure around the hood, along each side edge and the bottom edge of the cape. With the fur fibers hanging toward the bottom, cut enough 2¼"-wide strips of fur to equal the total measurement. Cutting the length and butting ends together as needed, glue 1" of the fur strips 1" from the edge on the right side of the fabric around the hood, along each side edge and the bottom edge of the cape. Fold the extended edge of the fur to the wrong side of the cape and glue in place.
12: Cut a piece of burgundy/metallic gold braided trim to fit along the inner edge of the fur around the cape and hood edges and glue in place, mitering the trim at each corner.
13: Cut a piece of burgundy/metallic gold braided trim to fit around the center of the body. With the ends at the back, glue the trim in place. Cut another piece of trim to fit down the center front, from the body center to under the head *(see photo)*; glue the trim in place.
14: For **Santa's bag,** fold the brown felt in half matching the 8" sides. Allowing ¼" for a seam, sew the sides together, forming a tube. At one end of the tube, run a gathering thread close to the edge. Pull the thread to tightly gather for the bottom and secure the thread; turn right side out.
15: Cut a 4" x 12" strip of quilt batting; roll tightly and insert into the bag, giving a full appearance.
16: At the bag opening, loosely gather the sides around the batting and glue the remaining velvet ribbon around the gathers, leaving about 7" for a handle. Fold the 7" length in half and glue the end to the bag.
17: Arrange the miniature teddy bear, violin and gift packages in Santa's bag *(see photo)*.
18: Bring the hands around to the front of the body; arrange and glue each hand to the body as desired.
19: Place the cape over Santa's head; glue the seam at the neck of the cape to the back of the head.
20: For the Christmas Tree, randomly glue the gold beads to the sisal Christmas tree. Glue the Tree in Santa's hand.

Glass Ornament Wreath
Continued from page 125

arranging as you go, using the wire cutters, trim each bamboo skewer to the desired length and push the skewer into the hole punched in the foam. Cover as much of the foam wreath as possible with the larger ornaments.
4: Trimming the bamboo skewer of each medium ornament so it sets above the larger ones, making starter holes and arranging as you go, push the bamboo skewers into the foam to fill in around the larger ornaments.
5: In the same manner as step 4, trim and arrange the smaller ornaments on the wreath.
6: Cut a 24"-long piece of ribbon; wrap the piece around the wreath and tie the ends in a knot at the front of the wreath.
7: For the **bow,** following the manufacturer's instructions for the bowmaker, or by hand, fold a 14"-wide multi-looped bow with 24" streamers; cut a 12" piece of foil wire and tightly wrap the center of all the loops and streamers; twist the ends together at the back to secure.
8: Over and around the knot of the tied ribbon, push the foil wire ends of the bow into the foam of the wreath.

❋ The Man Behind the Magic

The real St. Nicholas was born in 280 A.D. in Patara, a city in Asia Minor. He was a Christian priest who later became a bishop. He came from a wealthy family and traveled the country helping people and giving gifts of money and other presents. His gifts were given late at night, because he did not like to be seen when he gave them away.

A famous story about St. Nicholas involves a poor man who had no money to give to his three daughters on their wedding day. St. Nicholas dropped bags of gold into the stockings that the girls had left to dry by the fire. The sisters found the gold and ever since, children have hung up stockings on Christmas Eve, hoping they will be filled with presents by Christmas morning. Children were also told to go to sleep quickly or he would not come!

Victorian Christmas Boxes

Continued from page 123

- decorative embroidery stitches *(optional)*
- ❏ Embroidery needles and floss *(if not using sewing machine stitches)*
- ❏ Mauve pearl cotton
- ❏ Sewing needle and thread
- ❏ Pins
- ❏ Assorted buttons
- ❏ Tape measure or ruler
- ❏ Pencil
- ❏ Iron
- ❏ Large piece of paper
- ❏ Gem-Tac™ by Beacon™ or strong fabric glue
- ❏ Duro Spray Adhesive
- ❏ Hot glue gun and glue sticks

Instructions

1: With the spray paint, spray the inside and the outside of the bottom of each box; let dry. Add additional coats as needed for total coverage.

2: In the same manner, paint the inside of each box lid; let dry.

3: Cut each ¼ yd. piece of coordinating fabric into pieces in assorted sizes and irregular shapes *(see photo)*.

4: Lay each box lid on top of the large piece of paper; with the pencil, trace around the outer edge of the box lids for patterns. Cut out each pattern 2" larger on all sides than the outline of the box lid.

5: For a **base**, using each pattern, cut one from muslin fabric.

6: For each **crazy quilt top** *(make 2)*, beginning in the center of the muslin base, lay one irregular fabric piece in place. For the next fabric piece, matching one raw edge of the center fabric piece, lay a different piece of fabric facedown on top of the center piece. Allowing ¼" for seams, sew the two pieces together and to the muslin base. Unfold the top piece of fabric and press the seam flat. For the next fabric piece, in the same manner, lay another piece of fabric facedown along one edge of the center piece and sew together; unfold and press. Continue in this manner around all sides, sewing pieces together to cover the muslin base.

7: For the **decorative stitching,** thread the sewing machine with the desired embroidery thread and choose the desired stitch. Embellish the seams of the different fabric pieces with decorative stitching *(see photo)*, changing the stitch selection and the thread as desired, leaving a few seams plain for gluing metallic trim, if desired. If using the embroidery needle and floss, refer to your favorite embroidery instruction book for making desired stitches. If desired, thread the embroidery needle with mauve pearl cotton and work Herringbone Stitch along a seam according to the illustration.

HERRINGBONE STITCH

8: Following the manufacturer's instructions, spray the top of each box lid with spray adhesive. Lay the box lids adhesive side down on top of the foam batting; press with your hand to adhere the box lids and let dry. Trim away excess foam batting from each box lid.

9: Lay the crazy quilt top over the foam batting on the box lid, smoothing out any wrinkles. At the center, pin the quilt top to the foam batting. Pulling gently, but firmly taut, pin the quilt top to the foam batting around the outer edges. Smooth the edge of the quilt top over the edge of the box lid and trim the fabric even with the lid. Cutting and folding as needed, fit the fabric in each corner; with hot glue, glue the edge of the quilt top to the side edge of the box lid.

10: Cut several pieces of plain or metallic trim to fit around the edge of the box lid *(see photo)*. Glue each piece in place, overlapping rows as needed to cover the sides of the box lid.

11: For decorating the crazy quilt top, glue or sew the crochet doilies, assorted ribbon roses, flat crystals and pearls, charms, strung pearls, buttons, cutoff ends of trim and lace appliqués as desired to the fabric *(see photo)*; let dry.

12: Fold ½" under to the wrong side along one long edge of the piece of mauve moire taffeta fabric and the burgundy moire taffeta fabric.

13: Place the box lid on the appropriate box; with the pencil draw a line on the box bottom around the lid.

14: For the large box bottom sides, with the folded edge of the mauve fabric along the pencil line, glue the length of the fabric around the box sides; fold the end of the fabric under about ½" and glue the fold in place. Along the opposite edge of the fabric, fold to the bottom of the box, cutting as needed to fit over the corners. Repeat with the burgundy fabric for the small box bottom sides.

15: Cut a piece of braided trim to fit along the edge of the fabric on the bottom of each box and glue in place to hide the raw edge. Cut a second piece of braided trim to fit around the sides of each box and glue in place about ½" below the edge of the lid *(see photo)*.

Holiday Home ~ page 131

Christmas Floral Trio Set

Photo on pages 130 and 131

Swag

Finished Size:
About 20" across x 9" wide including trims.

Materials:
- 16" foam Swag with wire hanger loop by Plastifoam
- 25 green silk 3½"-wide x 5"-long magnolia leaves with stems removed
- 6 green silk 3½"-wide desired leaves with stems removed
- 2 large bunches of burgundy artificial grapes
- 8 floral picks with 6 gold berries each
- 5 gold 25 mm round plastic ornaments
- 4 pinecones each about 2" across
- 8 sprigs of artificial pine each about 4½" long
- 6 clusters of silk green hydrangea blossoms
- 15 stems of green eucalyptus
- Twisted satin cord:
    - 2½ yds of ½"-wide burgundy
    - 2½ yds of ¼"-wide dark purple
- 35 floral pins
- Gold spray paint
- Hot glue gun and glue sticks
- Wire cutting pliers

Instructions

1: With the spray paint, lightly spray each pinecone and magnolia leaf; let dry.

2: Beginning in the center of the foam swag, spread glue on the back of a magnolia leaf; lay it in place, and push a floral pin through the top of the leaf into the foam. In this manner, overlapping and arranging the leaves as you go, and reversing the direction of the leaves on the opposite side of center, glue and pin leaves to the swag to completely cover the foam *(see photo)*.

3: Pull six or eight grapes from the bunches and reserve for later.

4: For the center focal point, just to the right of center, with the side where grapes have been removed toward the swag, pin one large bunch of grapes to the swag, allowing the bottom to hang freely below the edge of the swag *(see photo)*. From underneath, glue the grapes in place on the swag.

5: Cut the remaining bunch of grapes into four pieces. Arranging as you go, pin and glue each piece to the swag around the large bunch of grapes *(see photo)*.

6: Trimming the ends of the eucalyptus stems to various lengths, arrange four stems above and to the right of the large bunch of grapes and four below and to the left of the large bunch of grapes, gluing each stem in place.

7: Glue the pinecones and the gold ornaments along the swag on each side of the center focal point.

8: Folding loops as desired with the twisted satin cord, arrange and glue the cord in and around the grapes, the pinecones and the gold ornaments.

9: Glue one of the reserved grapes over each cut end of the twisted cord.

10: Fill in around all the items on the swag with the gold berry picks, hydrangea blossoms, pine sprigs and remaining eucalyptus stems, gluing each additional item in place as needed.

Candle Centerpiece

Finished Size:
About 16" across x 9" high including trims.

Materials:
- 14" foam Beveled Wreath by Plastifoam
- 9"-high clear glass Cylinder Vase #4004 by Syndicated Sales, Inc.
- Small ivory floating candle
- Clear glass marbles to weight vase
- 30 green silk 3½"-wide x 5"-long magnolia leaves with stems removed
- 6 green silk 3½"-wide desired leaves with stems removed
- 7"-long bunch of burgundy artificial grapes
- 4"-long bunch of burgundy artificial grapes
- 8 picks with 6 gold berries each
- 4 gold 25 mm round plastic ornaments
- 4 pinecones each about 2" across
- 12 sprigs of artificial pine each about 4½" long
- 6 clusters of silk green hydrangea blossoms
- Twisted satin cord:
    - 3 yds. of ½"-wide burgundy
    - 3 yds. of ¼"-wide dark purple
- 12" of ½"-wide dark purple braided trim
- 35 floral pins
- Gold spray paint
- Hot glue gun and glue sticks
- Wire cutting pliers
- Water source

Instructions

1: With the spray paint, lightly spray each pinecone and magnolia leaf; let dry.

2: Spread glue on the back of a magnolia leaf and lay it in place on the beveled wreath, push a floral pin through the top of the leaf and into the foam. In this manner, overlapping and arranging the leaves in the same direction as you go, glue and pin leaves to the wreath to completely cover the foam *(see photo)*.

3: For the focal point, lay three of the remaining leaves on one area of the wreath; pin the tops in place together and fan out. Pin the large bunch of grapes to the wreath, allowing the bottom to hang freely *(see photo)*. From underneath, glue the grapes in place on the wreath.

4: Glue three of the pinecones and two of the gold ball ornaments to the wreath in and around the large bunch of grapes.

5: Cut a 36" piece of burgundy twisted cord and set it aside. With each of the remaining pieces of twisted cord, folding loops as desired, arrange the loops and glue the cord in and around the grapes, the pinecones and the gold ball ornaments.

6: Fill in around all the focal point items with the gold berry picks, pine sprigs and hydrangea blossoms, gluing each additional item in place as needed.

7: Opposite the focal point, pin the tops of any remaining leaves together and fan out. Pin and glue the smaller bunch of grapes to the wreath over the leaves. In the same manner as for the focal point, arrange the remaining items *(see photo)*.

8: Glue the braided trim around the vase *(see photo)*.
9: Place the marbles in the vase; fill the vase with water to the desired level. Place the vase in the center of the wreath and float the lighted candle on the water.

Topiary

Finished Size:
About 25" high.

Materials:
- 18" foam Cone by Plastifoam
- 6" terra cotta pot
- Americana® Acrylic Paints by DecoArt™:
    Dioxazin Purple #DA101
    Lt. Avocado #DA106
- 50 green silk 3½"-wide x 5"-long magnolia leaves with stems removed
- 5 variegated green silk 3½"-wide grape leaves with stems removed
- 3 large bunches of burgundy artificial grapes
- 15 floral picks with 6 gold berries each
- 20 sprigs of green silk boxwood each 3" long
- 8 sprigs of artificial pine each 4½" long
- 2 dark purple 3½"-long tassels
- Twisted satin cord:
    3 yds of ½"-wide burgundy
    3 yds of ¼"-wide dark purple
- 3 yds. of ½" wide dark purple braided trim
- 75 floral pins
- Gold spray paint
- Sea sponge
- Paint palette or foam plate
- 1"-wide foam brush
- Hot glue gun and glue sticks
- Wire cutting pliers

Instructions
1: With the foam brush and dioxazin purple, paint the outside of the terra cotta pot; let dry. Apply additional coats as needed for desired opaqueness.
2: Pour a little lt. avocado paint on the paint palette or foam plate; dip the sponge into the paint and lightly apply to the terra cotta pot, allowing the purple to show through in some areas.
3: Clean the sponge with water and let dry.
4: Spraying the sponge with gold spray paint and in the same manner as for the lt. avocado paint, apply gold paint to the terra cotta pot.
5: Cut a piece of purple braided trim to fit around the upper edge of the terra cotta pot; glue the piece in place.
6: With the gold spray paint, lightly spray each pinecone and magnolia leaf; let dry.
7: Spread glue on the back upper half of one magnolia leaf; beginning at the bottom, lay the leaf over the cone and pin in place at the top of the leaf. In this manner, overlap and arrange the leaves all in one direction in rows around the cone to completely cover the foam *(see photo)*.
8: Cut the bunches of grapes into smaller clusters. Pin a large cluster at the top of the leaf-covered cone *(see photo)*; glue the under side of the grape bunch to the cone. Arrange the remaining grape clusters around the sides of the cone, pinning and gluing in place.
9: Cut off two gold berries from the gold berry picks and a few leaves from a boxwood stem; set aside. Trimming the stems as needed and filling in as desired, arrange the pine sprigs, the boxwood sprigs, the gold berry picks, the eucalyptus stems and grape leaves, gluing each additional item in place as needed.
10: Cut each of the lengths of twisted cord in half. Beginning at the top of the cone, fold loops and drape each piece of cord as desired, gluing the loops in and around the items on the cone.
11: Glue one tassel to each end of the remaining piece of braided trim; glue a gold berry over the top of the tassel and a few of the boxwood leaves around the berry. Tie a bow at the center of the braided trim and glue the bow to the top of the cone. Arrange the bow loops and length of each streamer along the sides of the cone as desired and glue in place as needed.
12: Spread glue on the bottom of the cone; turn the terra cotta pot upside down and place the cone centered on the bottom of the pot.

Alternatives to Household Cleaners

Brass: Rub with a lemon half that has been dipped in salt.

Copper: Rub vigorously with a lemon half that has been dipped in a mixture of salt and white vinegar.

Crystal: Wash in a solution of one part vinegar to three parts water.

Glassware: Half fill a container with cold water and add one tablespoon of dry mustard, shake, leave for 30 minutes then rinse. You might also mix a grated peeled potato with warm water, allow the solution to stand in container, swirling occasionally, and rinse. Another alternative is to place raw rice, a dash of vinegar and salt with water in the container; swish, empty and then rinse.

Silver: Clean with a solution made from one and a half teaspoons of salt and one and a half teaspoons of bicarbonate of soda dissolved in one quart of water. Bring to a boil and drop silver cutlery in, boil for 3 minutes and then polish with a soft cloth. If the silver is badly tarnished, add a piece of heavy-duty aluminum foil.

Holiday Borders

Designed by Minette Collins Smith

Materials for One of Each:
- Velour Fingertip Towels with E-Z Stitch™ 14-count Aida insert by Charles Craft, Inc.:
    Cranberry #VT-69002405
    Evergreen #VT-69002907
    White #VT-69006750
- Six-Strand Embroidery Floss Art. 117 by DMC®:
    Colors listed in individual keys
- Size 24 tapestry needle

Instructions
For each towel, using two strands of floss for cross-stitches and backstitches as indicated on Key, center and stitch the design on the Aida insert of one towel according to the individual graphs.

Graphs continued on page 139

CROSS STITCH (X)

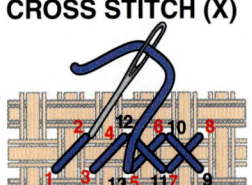

QUARTER CROSS STITCH (¼x)

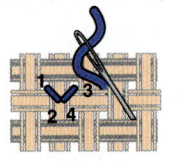

BACKSTITCH (B'st)

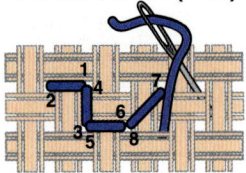

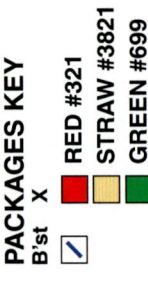

PACKAGES KEY
B'st X
RED #321
STRAW #3821
GREEN #699

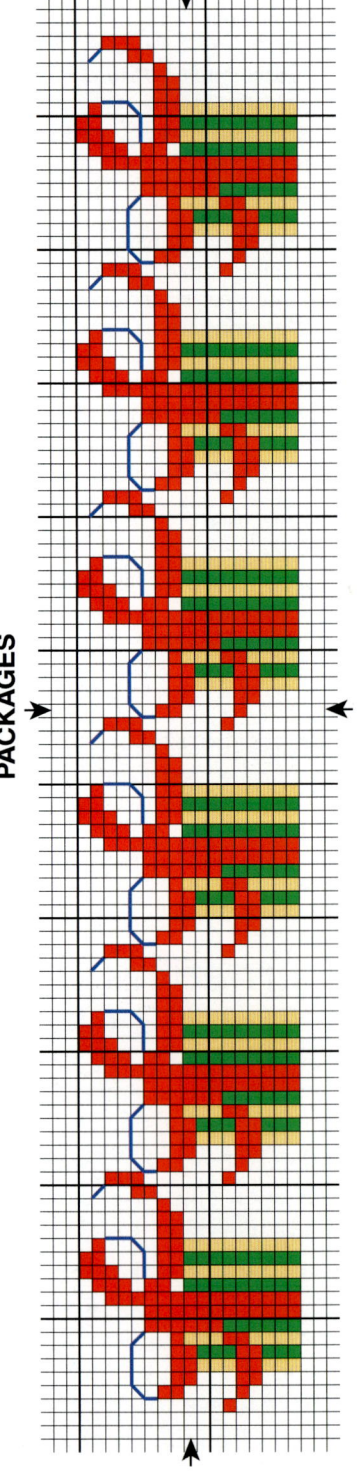

PACKAGES

Holiday Home ~ page 134

Victorian Stocking

Designed by Beth Wheeler

Finished Size:
10" x 15".

Materials:
- ½ yd. of cream with ecru print fabric
- ½ yd. of muslin fabric
- 1½ yds. of ½"-wide gold shirred rayon fabric piping
- Organza ribbon:
    - 3 yds. of ½"-wide metallic copper
    - 3 yds. of ½"-wide metallic gold
    - 3 yds. of 1¼"-wide white
    - 3 yds. of 1½"-wide metallic gold
    - 3 yds. of 1½"-wide metallic copper
    - 3 yds. of 2"-wide ivory
- Desired doilies — shown in photo are:
    - 3 new 4"-wide crochet doilies
    - 5½" x 12" piece of an old crochet doily
    - 3 crochet medallions
    - 2 metallic gold Battenburg lace doilies
- Desired buttons — shown in photo are:
    - 1 gold ⅞"-wide shank button
    - 22 assorted flat white buttons
- 6" of white 4 mm twisted cord
- Sewing machine (optional)
- Sewing needle
- Sewing thread to match fabrics
- Monofilament thread
- Tracing paper and pencil

Instructions

1: With the tracing paper and the pencil, trace the Stocking Pattern (see page 138). Extend the pattern lines 7" from where they end for the top edge; cut out.

2: For the outer stocking, with the traced pattern, cut one and one reversed from the cream print fabric; for the lining, cut two from the muslin fabric.

3: For the **stocking front,** arrange the doilies and the crochet medallions as desired on one outer stocking piece. When satisfied with the placement, use the monofilament thread to sew in place around the outer edge of each piece.

4: For the **piping trim,** with the raw piping edge to the outside, cutting to fit, pin the piping around the outer edge of the stocking front.

5: For the **hanger loop,** fold the twisted cord in half; on the right side of the fabric, match the cord ends with the top edge of the remaining outer stocking piece. Sew across the cord ends to secure.

6: With right sides together and matching edges, lay the remaining outer stocking piece over the stocking front; leaving the top edge open and allowing ½" for a seam, using matching thread, sew together around the sides. Turn the stocking right side out.

7: In the same manner as for the piping around the sides, pin the remaining piping in place around the top edge of the stocking and sew in place; fold the seam allowance to the inside.

8: For the **lining,** match the edges of the lining pieces; leaving the top edge open and allowing ½" for a seam, sew together around the sides. Do not turn.

9: Place the lining inside the stocking; fold the top edge seam allowance of the lining to the wrong side and match the fold with the piping edge. With the needle and thread, sew the lining in place.

10: With the needle and thread, sew the buttons to the stocking front as desired (see photo).

11: For a **concertina rose,** fold a 3 yd. piece of ribbon in half at an angle, forming a "V" (see step A on Concertina Rose Folding illustration). Fold one side over the width of the ribbon (see step B on illustration), then the other side (see step C on illustration), for the entire length of each ribbon half, leaving about 1" at each end. Holding the 1" ends, let go of the folds, the ribbon should look like accordion folds; holding one end of the ribbon tightly, pull the other end through your fingers (see step D on illustration); the ribbon will draw into a spiral, folding petals as you pull. From underneath, sew several times through all the folds to secure the shape of the rose; run the needle up through the center of all the folds. Place the concertina rose on the stocking where desired; run the needle down through the center of the rose and through the fabric underneath; run the needle up through the fabric and the center of the rose; do this several times to secure the rose to the stocking. Cut off the long ribbon tail.

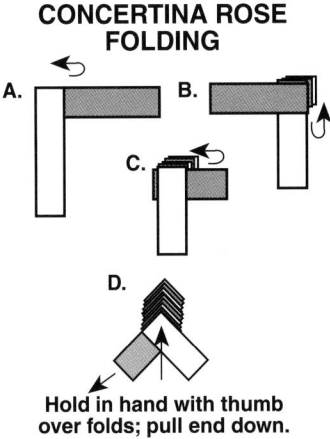

CONCERTINA ROSE FOLDING

Hold in hand with thumb over folds; pull end down.

12: With each remaining piece of organza ribbon, fold a concertina rose and secure it to the top edge of the stocking. Save the cut off pieces for other projects.

13: Place the gold shank button at the center of the white concertina rose and sew to the fabric underneath.

Victorian Stocking
Continued from page 137

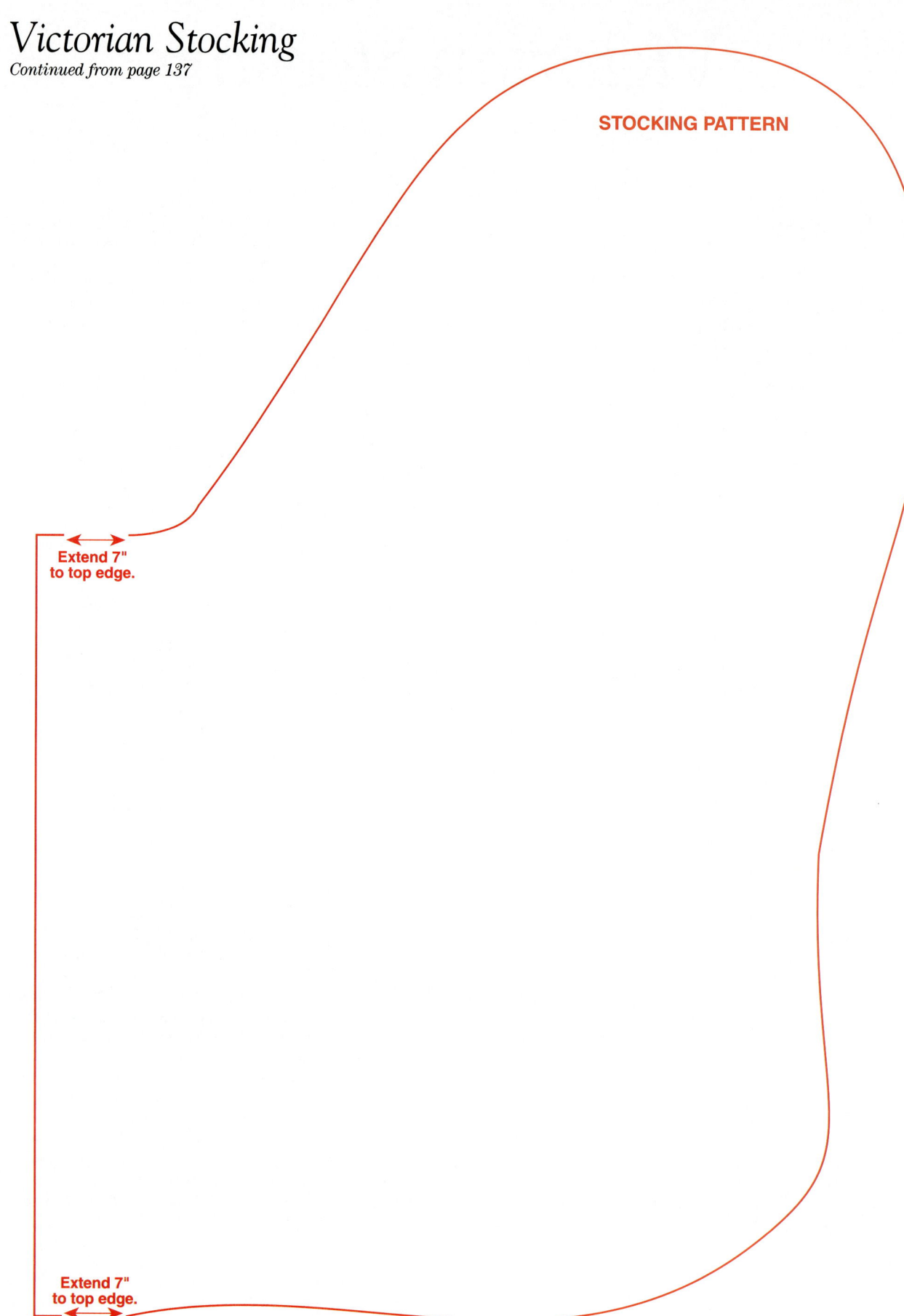

Holiday Borders
Continued from page 134

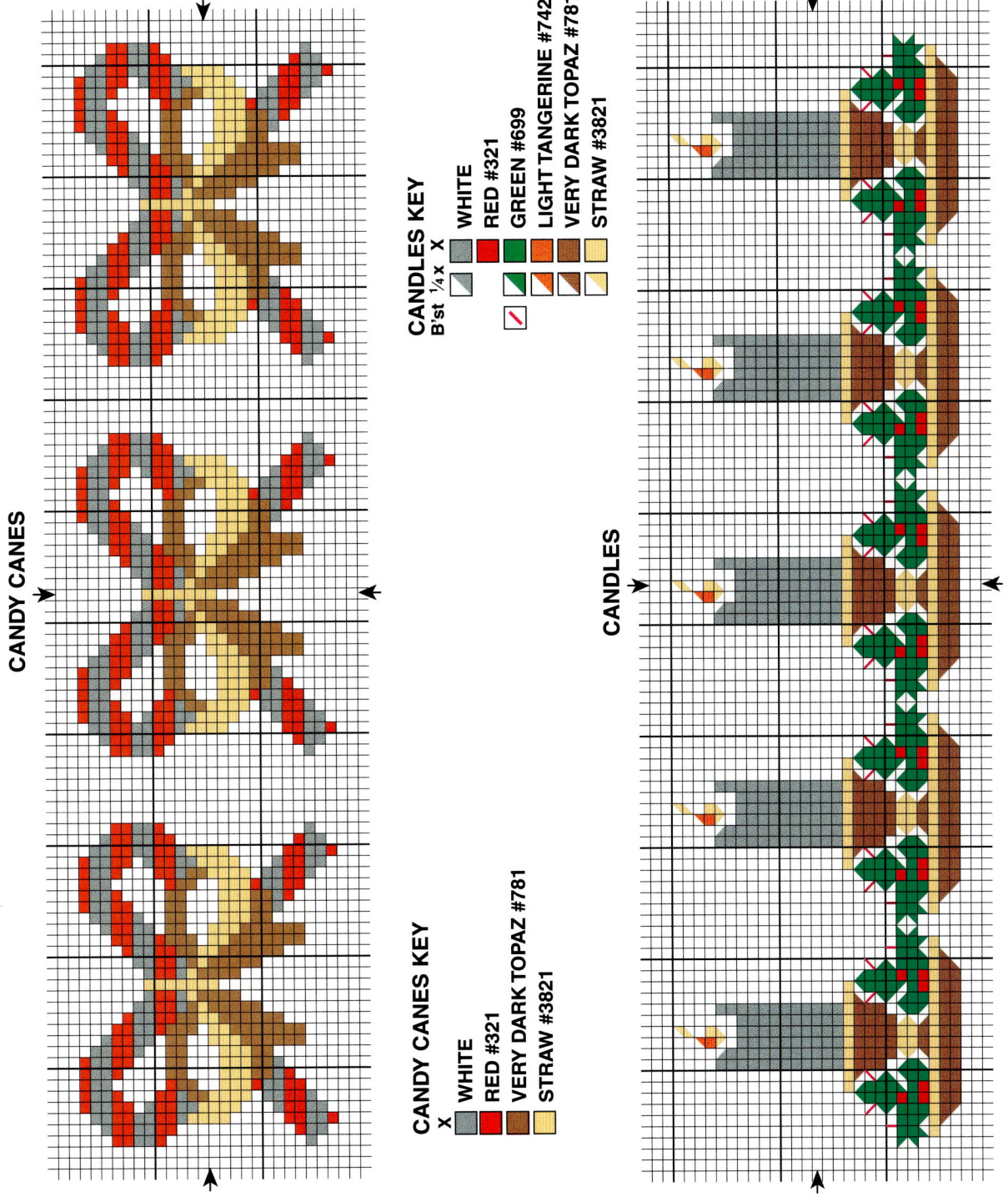

Kissing Ball

Designed by Wilma Bonner

Finished Size:
27" from top of hanger to bottom of tassel.

Materials for One:
- 100 yds. of white size 3 crochet thread
- Round 9" balloon
- 30" of ivory 6 mm strung pearls
- Desired silk floral items — shown in photo are:
    4 white 2" roses
    Several pieces of white wisteria
    Several pieces of green ivy
- 4 yds. of 1⅜"-wide Ivory Wire Edge Sheer Ribbon by Offray
- 6"-long white and gold tassel
- Straight pin
- Fabric stiffener
- Paintbrush
- Hot glue gun and glue sticks
- Size 2 steel crochet hook or hook needed to obtain gauge

Gauge: 8 dc = 1".

Basic Stitches: Ch, sl st, sc, dc. Refer to your favorite crochet instruction book for how to work stitches.

Crochet Cover
First Half
Rnd 1: Ch 5 *(counts as dc and ch 1)*, dc in fifth ch from hook, ch 1, (dc in same ch as last dc, ch 1) 10 times; join with sl st in fourth ch of ch-5. *(12 dc made)*

Rnd 2: Ch 7, sl st in fourth ch from hook *(first picot made)*; *(dc in next dc, ch 4, sl st in fourth ch from hook — *next picot made*); repeat from * around, join with sl st in third ch of ch-7. *(12 dc, 12 picots)*

Rnd 3: (Ch 3, 2 dc) in first dc, ch 5, skip next dc, (3 dc in next dc, ch 5, skip next dc) around, join with sl st in top of ch-3. *(18 dc, 6 ch-5 sps)*

Rnd 4: (Ch 3, dc) in first st, 2 dc in each of next 2 dc, ch 5, skip next ch-5 sp, (2 dc in each of next 3 dc, ch 5, skip next ch-5 sp) around, join.

Rnd 5: (Ch 3, dc) in first st, dc in next 4 dc, 2 dc in next dc, ch 5, skip next ch-5 sp, (2 dc in next dc, dc in next 4 dc, 2 dc in next dc, ch 5, skip next ch-5 sp) around, join.

Rnd 6: Ch 2, dc next 3 sts tog, ch 5, dc next 4 sts tog, ch 5, sc in next ch-5 sp, ch 5, (dc next 4 sts tog, ch 5, dc next 4 sts tog, ch 5, sc in next ch-5 sp, ch 5) around, skip ch-2, join with sl st in top of dc-3-tog. *(18 ch-5 sps)*

Rnd 7: Sl st in next 3 chs, ch 1, sc in ch-5 sp, ch 7, (sc in next ch-5 sp, ch 7) around, join with sl st in first sc. *(18 ch-7 sps)*

Rnds 8–9: Sl st in next 4 chs, ch 1, sc in ch-7 sp, ch 7, (sc in next ch-7 sp, ch 7) around, join.

Rnd 10: Sl st in next 4 chs, ch 3, (yo, insert hook in same st, yo, pull through 2 lps on hook) 2 times, yo, pull through all lps on hook *(first cluster made)*; ch 7, sc in next ch-7 sp, ch 7, *yo, insert hook in next st, yo, pull through st, yo, pull through 2 lps on hook, (yo, insert hook in same st, yo, pull through st, yo, pull through 2 lps on hook) 2 times, yo, pull through all lps on hook *(next cluster made)*; ch 7, sc in next ch-7 sp, ch 7; repeat from * around, join with sl st in top of first cluster. *(9 clusters, 9 ch-7 sps)*

Rnd 11: Sl st in next 4 chs, ch 1, sc in ch-7 sp, ch 7, (sc in next ch-7 sp, ch 7) around, join with sl st in first sc. Fasten off. *(18 ch-7 sps)*

Second Half
Rnds 1–11: Repeat rnds 1–11 of First Half. At the end of rnd 11, **do not fasten off.**

Rnd 12: Sl st in next 4 chs, ch 1, sc in ch-7 sp; holding both Halves with wrong sides together, ch 3, sc in any ch-7 sp on rnd 11 of First Half, ch 3, (sc in next ch-7 sp on Second Half, ch 3, sc in next ch-7 sp on First Half, ch 3) around, join. Fasten off.

Finishing
1: Following the manufacturer's instructions, saturate the Crochet Cover with fabric stiffener.
2: Insert the balloon through a chain space of the Cover; inflate the balloon to fit tightly inside and stretch the Cover snug. Tie off the balloon. With the paintbrush, remove excess stiffener; let dry.
3: Use the straight pin to pop the balloon; remove and discard the balloon.
4: For the **hanger,** glue one end of the strung pearls to rnd 11 on one Half; glue the opposite end of the pearls to rnd 11 on the other Half directly across from the first end.
5: For the **tassel,** run the tassel hanger loop through a joining chain space on the opposite side of the Cover directly below the hanger; run the tassel through the hanger loop and pull tight.
6: Cut the ribbon into two 1½ yd. pieces and one 1 yd. piece. With each 1½ yd. piece of ribbon, fold and tie a 7"-wide multi-loop bow with 4" streamers.
7: Glue the bows back-to-back around the tassel at the bottom.
8: Glue two roses side by side on each side of the hanger. Fold the 1 yd. of ribbon in half, glue the fold to the ball between the ends of the hanger; leaving 4" at each end for streamers, shape the ribbon into 3" loops and glue to the ball *(see photo)*.
9: At the top and the bottom of the ball, arrange and glue the wisteria and the ivy in and around the ribbon loops.

Christmas Books

Designed by Jean Ashley

Finished Sizes:
Sizes range from 8" wide x 11" high to 3½" wide x 5" high.

Materials:
- Paper maché book-shaped boxes:
    - ⅞" thick x 3⅝" wide x 5⅛" high *(smallest)*
    - 1⅜" thick x 4½" wide x 6⅜" high *(small)*
    - 1⅞" thick x 5½" wide x 7⅞" high *(medium)*
    - 2¼" thick x 6½" wide x 9½" high *(large)*
    - 2¾" thick x 8" wide x 10⅞" high *(largest)*
- Americana® Acrylic Paints by DecoArt™:
    - Antique White #DA58
    - Light Cinnamon #DA114
    - Deep Burgundy #DA128
    - Hauser Dark Green #DA133
    - Blue Violet #DA141
- Matte #DAS13 Americana® Sealer/Finisher by DecoArt™
- Dazzling Metallics™ Acrylic Paints by DecoArt™:
    - Glorious Gold #DA71
    - Champagne Gold #DA202
- Weathered Wood™ #DAS8 Crackling Medium by DecoArt™
- Gold paint pen
- Black paint pen
- ½"-wide flat paintbrush
- ¼"-wide flat paintbrush

Instructions

1: For the **base coat** on each book box, with champagne gold paint and the ½"-wide flat paintbrush, paint the outside cover and inner cover edge; let dry.

2: With glorious gold paint and the ½"-wide flat paintbrush, paint the inside of each book box and box lid; let dry. Add additional coats as desired for total coverage.

3: Following the manufacturer's instructions, apply crackle medium to the outside of each box; let dry.

4: For the **top coat** on each box, with the ½"-wide flat paintbrush, paint as follows:
   - **A:** For the largest book box, paint with hauser dark green paint.
   - **B:** For the large book box, paint with antique white paint.
   - **C:** For the medium book box, paint with blue violet paint.
   - **D:** For the small book box, paint with light cinnamon paint.
   - **E:** For the smallest book box, paint with deep burgundy paint.

5: With glorious gold paint and the ½"-wide flat paintbrush, paint all sides of the "pages" of each book box *(see photo)*; let dry.

6: With glorious gold paint and the ¼"-wide flat paintbrush, paint the raised areas on the spine of each book box *(see photo)*; let dry.

7: With the gold paint pen, centered on the front cover of each book box, write and let dry as follows:
   - **A:** On the largest book box in script letters:
       A Christmas Carol
   - **B:** On the large book box:
       The Nutcracker and the Mouse King
   - **C:** On the medium book box:
       The Twelve Days of Christmas
       Draw a small Christmas tree with a star on top above the first word *(see photo)*.
   - **D:** On the small book box in uppercase letters:
       A VISIT FROM SAINT NICHOLAS
       In smaller uppercase letters:
       CLEMENT C. MOORE
   - **E:** On smallest book box in script letters:
       Gift of the Magi

8: On the front cover of the large book box, use the black paint pen to rewrite on the left of each letter for shading; let dry.

9: With the gold paint pen, using all uppercase letters on the spine of each book box, write and let dry as follows:
   - **A:** On the largest book box:
       A CHRISTMAS CAROL
       CHARLES DICKENS
   - **B:** On the large book box:
       THE NUTCRACKER AND THE MOUSE KING
       E.T.A. HOFFMAN
   - **C:** On the medium book box:
       THE TWELVE DAYS OF CHRISTMAS
   - **D:** On the small book box:
       A VISIT FROM SAINT NICHOLAS
       CLEMENT C. MOORE
   - **E:** On the smallest book box:
       GIFT OF THE MAGI
       O. HENRY

10: Spray each of the painted book boxes with sealer/finisher; let dry.

Wooden Cross

Designed by Kenna Prior

Finished Size:
48" high x 35" across.

Materials:
- Unfinished wooden turned table legs:
    - 3 each 15½" long
    - 28" long
- Unfinished wooden medallion 4" x 4" x 1"-thick
- 3 pieces of wood each 1" x 4" x 4"
- 16 finishing nails each ¾"-long
- 4 "L" angle brackets each ½"-wide x 3½"-long
- Elmer's Professional Carpenter's Wood Filler
- 16 wood screws each ¾"-long
- Sawtooth hanger and screws (optional)
- Spray Paint by Krylon®:
    - Ivory Satin #3510
    - Pewter Gray #1606
- Several pieces of soft cloth
- Hammer
- Pencil
- Drill with drill bit slightly smaller than wood screws
- Screwdriver
- Wood glue
- Sandpaper

Instructions

1: For the **center medallion**, glue the three 1" x 4" x 4" pieces of wood together to form a block, spread glue on the back of the medallion and glue in place on the block; use finishing nails to hold the block and medallion securely.
2: For the **arms**, lay the four wooden table legs on the work surface according to the Cross illustration.
3: Using one bracket as a guide, mark the holes for attaching each bracket to the center medallion (see illustration).
4: Use the drill and drill bit to drill the holes for each bracket.
5: To **assemble** the Cross, spread glue on the flat end of each table leg and lay in place on the center medallion; with the screwdriver, place a wood screw in each hole of each bracket; let dry.
6: On the front of the Cross, following the manufacturer's instructions, spread wood filler in each area where an arm is joined to the center medallion; let dry. Use sandpaper to sand the wood filler smooth.
7: Spray the entire Cross with gray spray paint; let dry. Apply additional coats as needed for total coverage.
8: Spraying one small area at a time, spray the Cross with ivory spray paint; use a soft cloth to wipe away some of the ivory paint to expose the gray underneath. Repeat spraying and wiping on the remainder of the Cross.
9: If desired, use the drill and wood screws to attach the sawtooth hanger to the upper back of the center medallion.

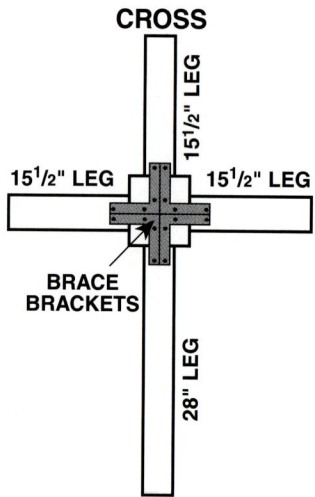

The Legend of the Dogwood Tree

When Christ was on earth,
the dogwood grew
To a towering size with lovely hue.
Its branches were strong and interwoven
And for Christ's cross its timbers
were chosen.
Being distressed at the use of this wood,
Christ made a promise which
still holds good:
"Not ever again shall the dogwood grow
To be large enough for such a tree,
and so
Slender and twisted it shall always be
With cross-shaped blossoms for all to see.
The petals shall have bloodstains
marked in brown
And in the blossom's center
a thorny crown.
All who see it will think of Me,
Nailed to a cross from the dogwood tree.
Protected and cherished
this tree shall be
A reflection to all of my agony."

Gold Nativity Set

Designed by Elizabeth Ann White

Finished Sizes:
From 1¾"-tall to 7"-tall.

Materials:
- 9 piece J-Porcelain Nativity Set by Wang's International, Inc.
- Classic Gold #6110 Liquid Leaf® by Plaid®
- Black #20504 Apple Barrel Colors® Acrylic Paint by Plaid®
- ½"-wide soft bristled flat paintbrush
- 1"-wide sponge paintbrush
- Soft cloth
- Assorted jewels — shown in photo are:
    Blue 3 mm x 5 mm oval cabochons
    Pearl 3 mm x 5 mm oval cabochons
    Red 6 mm x 8 mm faceted oval crystals
    Red 3 mm faceted round crystals
    Red 5 mm faceted round crystal
    Red 9 mm faceted star crystal
    Clear 5 mm x 10 mm faceted marquis crystals
    Green 5 mm x 10 mm faceted marquis crystals
    Green 3 mm faceted round crystals
    Blue 5 mm faceted round crystals
    Aqua 3 mm faceted round crystals
- Toothpicks
- E6000® by Eclectic Products, Inc. or strong craft glue

Instructions

1: With gold paint and the soft bristled paintbrush, paint the entire surface of each figurine of the porcelain nativity set; let dry. Add additional coats as need for desired opaqueness.

2: For the antiqued look, on each painted figurine, using the sponge brush, apply black paint to a small area; quickly before the paint dries, wipe with the soft cloth to remove paint from the smooth surface, leaving black in the detail crevices; let dry.

3: Around the base of each figurine, reapply gold paint; let dry.

4: For the jewels, with a toothpick, apply a tiny bit of glue on the back and place the jewel glue-side down on the figurine as shown in the photo or as desired; let dry.

Christmas Doormat

Designed by Marilyn Shelton

Materials:
- 18½" x 29" cocoa fiber doormat
- Weather-proof Wire Edge Ribbon by Wrights®:
    Spool of 2"-wide Red #222-2186-065
    Spool of 2"-wide Hunter Green #222-2186-925
- 1" square Velcro® Fastener
- E-Z Bowmaker *(optional)*
- 4" of Gold Quick Snip™ Foil Wire by FibreCraft®
- Crafty® Magic Melt® Floral Pro™ Glue Gun by Adhesive Technologies, Inc.
- Crafty® Magic Melt® Glue Sticks by Adhesive Technologies, Inc.

Instructions

1: Cut a 16" piece each of red ribbon and hunter green ribbon; lay the green ribbon on top of the red ribbon with about ½" of the red ribbon showing underneath *(see photo)*; lay the ribbons over one corner of the doormat, wrapping the ends to the back. At the side edge of the doormat, run a bead of glue under the red ribbon and adhere it to the green ribbon; run a bead of glue under the green ribbon and adhere it to the doormat.

2: Cut a 25" piece each of red ribbon and green ribbon; layer the ribbons in the same manner as before and on the opposite corner from the 16" pieces of ribbon, lay in place and glue as in step 1.

3: Following the manufacturer's instructions, with the bowmaker, or by hand, fold a 5"-high x 10"-wide, multi-looped bow with 10" streamers. Wrap the center of the loops with the foil wire, twisting the ends together at the back.

4: Glue half of the Velcro fastener to the back of the bow and the other half to the center of the 25" ribbons at the corner.

5: Attach the bow to the doormat.

Poinsettia Glass Clings

Designed by Kenna Prior

Finished Sizes:
Large Poinsettia measures 6¾" across; each Small Poinsettia measures 5½" across.

Materials:
- Gallery Glass® Black #16025 Simulated Liquid Leading™ by Plaid®
- Gallery Glass® Window Color™ by Plaid®:
    Ruby Red #16015
    Emerald Green #16009
    Kelly Green #16008
    Amethyst #16014
    Amber #16020
- 8" x 10" sheet of glass
- Glass cleaner
- Paper towels
- Tracing paper and pencil
- Masking tape

Instructions
1: Clean the sheet of glass with the glass cleaner and paper towels.
2: Trace the Large Cling pattern and the Small Cling pattern *(see pages 159 and 160)* onto tracing paper.
3: Tape the traced patterns to one side of the glass sheet.
4: Following the manufacturer's instructions, apply liquid leading to the glass following the lines on the paper pattern; all leading lines should touch to form areas for placing window color. Let the liquid leading dry about 72 hours until cured.
5: Following the manufacturer's instructions, apply window color inside the leading areas according to the key given for the patterns.

Continued on page 159

Victorian Christmas Wall Hanging

Designed by Phyllis Dobbs

Finished Size:
19" high x 19¾" wide.

Materials:
- 14" square of gold mesh fabric
- ½ yd. of red fabric
- 20" square of white muslin fabric
- Fabric:
    - ¼ yd. of green/metallic gold Christmas-print
    - 8" square of different Christmas-print
- 20" square of Warm and Natural® Soft & Bright™ Quilt Batting by The Warm™ Company
- 8" square of HeatnBond® Lite Iron-on Adhesive by Therm O Web
- 1 yd. of ⅝"-wide Forest Green Taffeta Wire Edge Ribbon by Offray
- Trims by Wrights®:
    - 8" of ½"-wide Metallic Gold Cluney Lace
    - 3" Metallic Gold Tassel
    - 2" Red Tassel
- Santa Claus Ceramic Button by Mill Hill
- Present Ceramic Button by Mill Hill
- 9 red 6 mm x 10 mm glass beads
- Assorted buttons:
    - 8 red ½"-wide flat
    - 3 red ⅝"-wide flat
    - 3 red ⅞"-wide flat
    - Green 1"-wide flat
    - Green ½"-wide flat
    - Green ¾"-wide flat
    - 4 gold ⅝"-wide metal flat
    - 1"-wide star-shape shank-style
- Red sewing thread
- Green sewing thread
- Monofilament or invisible sewing thread
- Sewing machine
- Sewing needle
- Iron
- Straight pins
- Tracing paper and pencil

Instructions

1: Cut a 14" square from the red fabric.

2: For the wall hanging **front,** layer the gold mesh fabric on the right side of the red fabric square. With monofilament thread, sew ¼" from the edge around the outside of the fabric squares.

Continued on page 157

Poinsettia Flower Box

Designed by Phyllis Sandford

Finished Size:
About 8" wide x 15" long x 11" high.

Materials:
- 5½"-wide x 15"-long x 7½"-wide wooden box
- Delta Ceramcoat® Acrylic Paints by Delta Technical Coatings, Inc.:
    - Lima Green #2072
    - Lisa Pink #2084
    - Black Green #2116
    - Mendocino Red #2406
    - Alpine Green #2439
    - White #2505
- Red Copper #2605 Gleams Ceramcoat® Acrylic Paint by Delta Technical Coatings, Inc.
- Gloss #07 003 0200 Interior/Exterior Varnish by Delta Technical Coatings, Inc.
- Color Float #07 006 0200 by Delta Technical Coatings, Inc. *(color float medium)*
- Copper #061030669 Renaissance™ Foil Kit by Delta Technical Coatings
- Brush Tub® #383 by Loew-Cornell *(water container)*
- La Corneille® Paintbrushes by Loew-Cornell®:
    - 10/0 Script Liner Series 7050
    - Size 6 Shader Series 7300
    - Size 8 Shader Series 7300
    - 1"-wide Wash/Glaze Series 7150
- Old toothbrush or paint spattering tool
- Water source
- Disposable paint palette or foam plate
- Paper towels
- Tracing paper
- Pencil
- White transfer paper
- Silk Poinsettia Bushes by A. C. Moore:
    - 2 White
    - 3 Fuchsia
    - 3 Pink
- Styrofoam® block to fit inside wooden box

Instructions

1: For the flower box, with the wash/glaze paintbrush and mendocino red, paint the entire outside of the wooden box; let dry. Apply additional coats as needed for total coverage.

2: Trace the Poinsettia pattern onto tracing paper and cut out.

3: For the center flower, lay the white transfer paper over

Continued on page 156

Poinsettia Flower Box
Continued from page 154

POINSETTIA

the center of one long side of the flower box with the traced pattern on top. Use the pencil to redraw the pattern lines to transfer the lines to the flower box.

4: For the flowers on each side of the center flower, move the pattern to the right or left of the center and turn to angle the petals a little differently from the center flower; transfer the pattern lines.

5: With white paint and the size 8 shader brush, fill in the outline of each petal on each flower.

6: Following the manufacturer's instructions, mix the color float medium with water in the water container.

7: Pour small amounts of mendocino red paint, white paint and lisa pink paint onto the paint palette.

8: For a three dimensional look, dip the size 8 shader in the color float medium; side load *(see Side Load illustration)* the longer bristles with mendocino red; make a few blending strokes on the palette to blend the paint with color float. On each flower, using the photo for reference, holding the brush with the paint color toward the area to be shaded, apply paint at the center where the petals join and along the edges of the petals for shadows; let dry.

9: For the **center veining,** mix white paint with mendocino red and lisa pink paints in three separate areas on the palette for three different shades: a light white/pink, a medium white/pink and light white/red. With color float medium, thin a little of each of the three different paint shade mixtures; using the photo for reference, load the liner brush and paint using the three different shades, applying the darker shade at the center, working outward with each of the next lighter shades; let dry.

10: For the **petal highlights,** side load the size 6 shader brush with color float medium and the lightest paint shade mixture; with the color along the outer edge, outline the petals you want to look as if on "top"; let dry. In the same manner, continue working toward the "back" shading the petals with the darkest paint shade mixture; let dry.

11: Thin a little alpine green paint with color float medium; load the liner brush and paint highlights on the "top" leaves.

12: For **the center** of each flower, dip the end of the handle of a shader brush into lima green paint; at the center of each flower, touch the end of the brush to the surface five or six times to make dots. Let dry.

13: For **the highlight** on each center dot, dip the handle end of the liner brush into red copper paint; touch the center of each green dot; let dry.

14: For each **pine bough** *(14 are shown on box in photo)*, thin a little black green paint with water and load the liner brush; for the stem, begin at the edge of one petal and pull the brush toward the outer edge of the box to

SIDE LOAD: Wet brush with water; pick up thinned color on one side of bristles.

the desired length.

15: For **the needles,** load the liner brush with thinned black green paint; beginning at the base and painting along each side of the stem, pull shorter strokes out to the desired length. Thin a little alpine green paint and red copper paint; continue painting needles on top of the black green needles with each color of thinned paint; let dry.

16: For the **white spatters,** thin a little white paint with water and choose one of the following:

A: If using the old toothbrush, dip the bristles into the thinned paint; hold the brush with the bristles up; pulling toward you, scrape your finger nail or a toothpick across the bristles to splatter paint on the box side. Turn the box and paint spatters on all sides; let dry.

B: Dip the spatter tool in the paint; holding the tool above the surface to be painted, turn the handle at the

Continued on page 160

Victorian Christmas Wall Hanging

Continued from page 153

3: With the tracing paper and pencil, trace the Tree Pattern *(see page 157)* and cut out.

4: Following the manufacturer's instructions, use the iron to adhere the iron-on adhesive to the wrong side of the 8" square of Christmas-print fabric.

5: For the **tree appliqué,** using the Tree Pattern, cut one from the prepared fabric. Remove the protective backing from the appliqué and with the iron, fuse the appliqué to the wall hanging front, referring to the photo for placement. Using green thread, sew a decorative zig-zag stitch around the outer edge of the appliqué.

6: Pin the gold lace in place on the wall hanging front, matching one end with the edge of the tree appliqué *(see photo)*. Do not sew at this time.

7: With the ribbon tie a 6"-wide bow, leaving the ends for streamers; referring to the photo for placement and folding the streamer ends under, pin the bow in place on the wall hanging front. Using green thread and tiny invisible stitches, remove the pins as you go and sew around all the edges of the ribbon to attach the bow to the fabric.

8: If desired, in groups of three buttons each, use red thread and sew a group of buttons to the wall hanging front at each end of the ribbon; sew another group near the bow *(see photo)*.

9: For **the border,** cut 3½"-wide strips from the ¼ yd. of Christmas-print fabric: two 14"-long and two 20"-long. Allowing a ¼" seam allowance, sew one 14"-long strip along the top of the front and the other along the bottom. In the same manner, sew one 20"-long strip along each side of the front.

10: Matching the edges, layer the wall hanging front with the quilt batting and the muslin fabric. With a needle and thread, beginning at the center and working out to the edge of the fabrics, baste through all layers of fabric 153to secure.

11: For the **quilting,** using invisible thread and sewing about ⅛" from the edge, sew around the inside edge of the border. In the same manner, quilt around the tree appliqué, the ribbon and the button groups.

12: Cutting through all the layers at the same time, trim around the edges of the quilted piece.

13: For the **binding,** from the remaining red fabric, cut enough 2"-wide strips that when sewn together end-to-end, will go around the outer edge of the quilted piece; sew the strips together.

14: Folding in half as you go, press the binding strip; unfold, then fold each long edge into the center fold and press again, forming a ½"-wide folded strip.

15: At the center of one side of the quilted piece, with right sides together, match the raw edges of the binding strip with the muslin back of the quilted piece; begin sewing the strip in place, stopping ¼" from the first corner; **to miter the corner,** match the binding strip with the edge of the quilted piece, fold the binding at an angle even with the edge and take one stitch; fold the binding back into place matching the edges and continue sewing, mitering each corner; cut the binding strip about ½" longer than needed to finish going around the edge and fold under and finish sewing the binding in place.

16: Refold the binding strip as pressed, wrapping the width of the strip around the edge of the quilted piece to the front; sewing close to the fold, sew the binding in place around the edge, mitering each corner the same as before.

17: For the embellishments:

A: For each **tassel,** sew the hanger loop to the wall hanging front where desired *(see photo)* and sew a button on top.

B: For the **beads** along the top of the gold lace trim, thread the needle with a single strand of red sewing thread and knot the end. Run the needle up through the lace from underneath; take a tiny stitch through the lace and the fabric; thread a bead on the needle and about the length of the bead, take another tiny stitch through the fabric; continue stitching and threading on beads the length of the lace.

C: For the Santa Claus button, sew in place on one bow streamer.

D: For the Present button, sew in place on the tree appliqué.

E: For the **button tassel** at the tree top, thread the needle with a single strand of green thread and tie a knot at the end. Run the needle up through the fabric at the top of the appliqué, thread one ½"-wide red flat button, take a tiny stitch, pulling the thread to allow the button to hang freely about 1" from the top of the tree and take another tiny stitch. In this manner, sew six more ½"-wide red flat buttons to the top of the tree appliqué; secure the thread.

F: Sew the green ½"-wide flat button on top of all the tiny stitches at the top of the tree appliqué; secure the thread.

G: Sew the green 1"-flat button, the star-shaped button and a ⅞"-wide red flat button in a three button group at the top left corner. ❈

TREE PATTERN
Cut 1 from Christmas-print fabric.

Finished Sizes:
Lengths range from 7" to 25" long.

Materials:
- ❏ 2 yds. of Gold Moroccan Braid by Offray
- ❏ 24" of Hunter Green & Burgundy Beaded Braid by Offray
- ❏ 2 Acrylic Crystal 20 mm Ball Drops #429-84 by Mangelsen's
- ❏ 4 Acrylic Crystal 32 mm Diamond Drops by Mangelsen's
- ❏ 6 Plated Flat Ripple Beads #06208-1-45 by Darice®
- ❏ Craft & Floral Pro™ Glue Gun by Adhesive Technologies, Inc.
- ❏ Crafty® Magic Melt® Glue Sticks by Adhesive Technologies, Inc.

Beaded Braid Tassel
At each end of the beaded braid, thread a ripple bead over the braid end with the flared bottom of the bead toward the end of the braid; glue one ball drop to the end of the braid. Spread glue around the end of the braid and pull the ripple bead over the glue and the top of the ball drop.

Gold Braid Tassel
1: Cut a 20" piece of gold braid.
2: In the same manner as for the beaded braid tassel, at each end of the gold braid, run the end through a ripple bead and glue a diamond drop with a ripple bead on the top.

Gold Braid Bow Tassel
1: Tie a multi-looped bow with the remaining gold braid.
2: In the same manner as for the beaded braid tassel, at each end of the gold braid, run the end through a ripple bead and glue a diamond drop with a ripple bead on the top. ❦

Poinsettia Glass Clings
Continued from page 151

SMALL CLING

- ■ RUBY RED
- ■ EMERALD GREEN
- ■ KELLY GREEN
- ■ AMETHYST
- ■ AMBER
- ▢ LEADING LINES

Continued on page 160

Poinsettia Glass Clings
Continued from page 159

LARGE CLING

■ RUBY RED
■ EMERALD GREEN
■ KELLY GREEN
■ AMETHYST
■ AMBER
□ LEADING LINES

❋ The Symbols of Christmas

Ornaments
The first Christmas trees had real fruit and flowers as their only ornaments. Cookies, nuts and other kinds of food were later added. Lighted candles were placed on the trees. In later years, German glass blowers began producing feather-weight glass balls to replace the fruit and other heavy ornaments.

Mistletoe
Mistletoe was sacred to ancient druids and a symbol of eternal life. The Romans valued it as a symbol of peace and this led eventually to its acceptance among Christmas props. Kissing under mistletoe was a Roman custom, too.

Poinsettia Flower Box
Continued from page 156

end of the brush to apply. Turn the box and paint spatters on all sides; let dry.
17: Following the manufacturer's instructions, apply foil adhesive from the kit around the top edge of the flower box; let dry.
18: For the **foiling**, lay a sheet of foil over the adhesive with the dull side down; rub your finger over the backing of the foil, releasing the foil onto the adhesive. Remove the sheet and lay it over another area of adhesive and rub. Continue around the top of the flower box rubbing foil over all the adhesive.
19: Place the Styrofoam block in the flower box.
20: Arrange the silk poinsettia bushes as desired, pushing the stem of each bush into the foam. ❋